Jim,

Kindest Regards

Many "Buzz" Shank

7-10-14

YES, I WAS THERE

A Perspective on
General Meade's Leadership
and the Battle of Gettysburg

William "Buzz" Shank

Layout and design by
Penny Maxson

S/P

Sluser Publishing

Printed in the USA

ISBN 978-0-578-12986-0

Original cover art
given to the author
by the late Charles Stoner

Cover redesigned by
Penny Maxson

~ Cover photos ~
Standing portrait: Mathew Brady
Sitting portrait: Library of Congress

S/P

Sluser Publishing
P.O. Box 6
Fayetteville, PA 17222

Dedication

This book is dedicated to my wife
Margaret Shank
and my children
Mary Beth Shank
Kevin Tanger
David Tanger

Foreword

General George Gordon Meade, Commander in Chief, Army of the Potomac during the Civil War, has finally received his just recognition under the pen of William "Buzz" Shank.

Historians have downplayed Meade's accomplishments during the period that changed the course of American history in favor of the more flamboyant commanders of the war. But the author's meticulous research of history has rectified the omission of Meade's contributions to the efforts of the North.

To be sure, Meade had the capacity of surrounding himself with capable and trusted subordinates, who without question followed his leadership and commands. This led to the Northern Army's victory at Gettysburg and the eventual defeat of the Southern forces, resulting in the preservation of the Union.

Meade, born in Spain, moved to Philadelphia with his parents at a tender age and was accepted at West Point at the age of 15. He graduated on July 1, 1835. Meade was assigned to the Topographical Engineers and reported to Texas in 1845 where he served in the Mexican War.

A modest servant, Meade rose through the ranks slowly as compared to others who trumpeted their accomplishments where it was most accepted, before politicians whose recommendations meant rapid advancement in the ranks. Meade was Lincoln's third choice to receive command of the Army of the Potomac.

Lincoln's reluctant choice of Meade, however, proved to be the deciding factor in the Civil War, and the preservation of the Union.

Robert V. Cox

General George G. Meade

Chapter 1

"Yes, I was there," the tall wiry man exclaimed. "You see, I grew up in Pennsylvania. To come to this place was not only a large responsibility, but an added incentive was instilled in those who called this land . . . . . home."

He must have spoken in quiet tones as his eyes reflected the excitement and sorrow that he had encountered in his home state just a short while ago. Maybe the reality of the events still had not settled into his inner thoughts. The enormity of what had transpired in one week was more than anyone could hope to comprehend in such a short period of time.

Yet this man may have contributed far more to the preservation of the Union during the Civil War than most people are willing to submit on his behalf. Those in control of the government at the time downplayed his accomplishment. Historians seem to have allowed his achievements to slip through the cracks in the annals of history. Nevertheless, what was accomplished against great odds and hardships by Meade remains a vital part of the history of the Civil War. Major General George Gordon Meade was Commander in Chief, Army of the Potomac, during a crucial period - June 28 through July 4, 1863 - a time that changed the course of American history.

Perhaps the time that served as a backdrop for Meade's golden hours could be classified as one of the more noble and soul-searching times that any nation has endured in human history.

The years between 1861 to 1865 - the Civil War years - were characterized by men of great bravery, courage, and commitment to a cause. To say that their individual experiences were the highlight of their lives is not too strong a statement for most of them. In the midst of this titanic conflict, two armies met around a quiet Pennsylvania crossroad town called Gettysburg. The impact of those forces would reshape these United States forever.

The Army of Northern Virginia was led by the brilliant General Robert E. Lee. His men were veteran, courageous, well rested, and determined to be victorious north of the Mason Dixon Line.

In contrast, the Army of the Potomac was headed by Meade, who just three days prior to the start of the conflict, was awakened at 4 a.m. and given command of the Northern forces, men who were accustomed to failure. Although there were certainly veterans among these demoralized troops, the leadership was scanty and ineffective. The lack of strong leadership started with the commanding generals and rose in an upward spiral through the War Department, the Congress, and on to the very top. Given this grotesque situation, Meade was expected to produce and develop a minor miracle. That is in fact, what Meade accomplished.

Many historians have chronicled the sequence of mistakes Lee made during the three day battle. Many feel comfortable in passing off these failures by saying Lee was unwell, and his orders were misinterpreted, and so the Army of Northern Virginia was defeated. Possibly it would be more to the point to concentrate on the positive steps Meade, the victorious commander, made that resulted in victory for the North, thus playing a major role in saving the Union. The efforts of Meade and his close advisors deserve much recognition.

From Gettysburg to Appomattox, the progress of the Southern forces continued downhill, a slide that eventually ended in surrender. On July 4, 1863, after Meade's decisive victory at Gettysburg, this must have been a clear possibility in Lee's mind. The will and determination of those brave men was sapped at Gettysburg. Their resolve was but a shadow of that of the troops who had so confidently marched into Pennsylvania, determined to win the war for the cause of the South.

The Battle of Gettysburg came as close as any major Civil War engagement at its beginning to being an encounter between even numbers of men and equipment. On the first and second days, the Army of Northern Virginia had a decisive edge in numbers, and this continued until late in the afternoon on the second day, when Major General John Sedwick's Sixth Corps arrived at Gettysburg to flesh out the Army of the Potomac. This would be the last battle of the war fought under these more-or-less equal conditions.

Under the soon-to-be-appointed General Ulysses S. Grant, the Union troops would hereafter be superior in both equipment and supplies. In addition, future Union forces would be superior to the Confederate ones by at least a two-to-one margin.

Back in Gettysburg, and with the men and equipment available to him, Meade, with the help of his trusted friends and generals, did what was best for the Union cause. Battles in this war were not generally decisive in nature; the defeated army was never completely dissolved. Yet, in Gettysburg, for a few short days, the Army of the Potomac faced the greatest general and the finest army ever assembled. By doing what had to be done, Meade and his army not only survived the conflict, but turned the tables on the Army of Northern Virginia and set into place the factors necessary for the ultimate victory of the North, and the preservation of the Union.

Chapter 2

By June of 1863, Lee was truly the star of the war. A handsome West Point graduate, Lee turned down the invitation of President Abraham Lincoln to take command of all the Union forces at the outset of the war. Lee remained loyal to the South and in mid-1862 received command of the Confederate Army. From this time forward, Lee and his troops experienced success after success, victory after victory.

The calculating President not only became embittered against his generals, with the exception of Grant, but his popularity was at a low ebb with the citizenry of the North. He needed a victory at all costs. The slaves had been emancipated on January 1, 1863, causing additional disruptions.

The giants of the European continent were growing restless. They needed and wanted the cotton from the South. Some felt perhaps they should intervene on behalf of the Rebel cause.

Into this scenario came a quiet, humble man, a man who allowed his military actions on the field of battle to speak for his cause. Meade, by being precise and expecting as much from his men as from himself, brought a new breed of command to the Army of the Potomac. Meade was a fighter, a man of wisdom, of courage, and one who would not be aroused into fright and mistakes.

In the battle around Gettysburg, one side would be victorious while the other would face the humbling experience of defeat. At Gettysburg, Lee tasted defeat after his impressive string of successes. He was outsmarted at his own game, while Meade implemented his plan for success. He did not deviate. He did not relent. He simply turned the tide of the war for the North. One is reminded of Isaiah 30:15, *"In quietness and in confidence shall be your strength."*

Bruce Catton, noted Civil War historian, described Meade in this way: *"The Pennsylvania troops were beginning to know George Gordon*

Meade, even though he was as yet only a brigadier, and a new one to boot. He was a tall grizzled man with a fine hawk's nose and a perfectly terrible temper, which would lash out furiously at any officer who failed to do his job."

A war correspondent said that Meade, on horseback, *"looked like a picture of a helmeted knight of old."* One of his staff complained that he rode in a most aggravating way, neither at a walk nor a gallop but at a sort of amble.

Meade was notably cool under fire. Often he sat on horseback, surrounded by his staff while viewing a battle through his field glasses. The action was intense with Rebel bullets whizzing by from all directions. This made his staff become impatient and want Meade to complete his reconnaissance so they could move to a safer haven. Eventually, he would put down his field glasses, and they would move to a safer location.

He never drew the kind of cheers that General George B. McClellan and General Joseph Hooker received, but he kept his command in good shape and had a sharp eye for details. When he reached a high place in the army, he did his job to the best of his ability and indulged in no argument or complaint when promotion and praise passed him by.

As the Civil War commenced, Meade was serving on a survey of the Great Lakes. He received a Volunteer's Star during the summer of 1861 and was assigned to the Division of the Pennsylvania Reserves. After their training and service near Washington and northern Virginia, the command joined the Army of the Potomac on the Peninsula. He fought at Beaver Dam Creek and Gaine's Mill before falling at Glendale. His injury there would be one that would trouble him the rest of his career and indirectly cause his death. A ball entered just above his hip joint, indented his liver, and passed out near his spine. Another ball hit his arm. He stayed with his horse, directed his charges and was forced to quit only through loss of blood. From that time on, Meade's hat was riddled by bullets, his mounts were killed, and his leg numbed by a shell, but he was never again wounded.

Meade led his brigade at Second Bull Run and the division at South Mountain and Antietam, where he won distinction. At Antietam, he succeeded the wounded Hooker as commander of the First Corps and received his second star before

Fredericksburg. There Meade's men broke through the Confederate right, but were thrown back when support failed to arrive. Next he took command of the Fifth Corps. Briefly Meade commanded the Grand Division after the Mud March until they were disbanded. Again, at Chancellorsville, he led his corps in fine fashion, however, he was held back by Hooker's timidity.

Meade handled troops well. He knew all aspects of engineering, had good tactics, and was courageous. He was the only officer in the Union forces who rose to great distinction during the war who was not reassigned from the army in 1861 when the war commenced.

Meade was neither a glamorous individual nor a braggart. Unfortunately, these were prerequisites in the Civil War if one was to advance and be successful on the Union side. Today, Meade would be called a *"working man's general."*

Good to his troops, he was one who expected and strived for perfection. He was the one who constantly checked positions and this guaranteed the safety of his men. In addition, the Civil War relied heavily on engineering skills. If you were a good engineer, it was an asset. Meade was a good engineer.

Grant said of Meade, *"His engineering proclivity clung to him throughout his career."* Grant, in this very generous estimate he makes of Meade, adds

" he saw clearly and distinctly the position of the enemy and the topography of the country in front of his position." Meade was also a man fiercely loyal to his superiors. It has been said, and rightly so, that even in the bad times, his loyalty to Hooker and others remained steadfast. There was another factor that placed Meade in a position from which he would never be able to gain his rightful place and recognition - President Lincoln. Through mid-June 1863, the President, for whatever reason, seemed to be experiencing a run of bad luck; he had no positive results from his generals in command. He felt that with the power that the North possessed, things should be going better. Lee had not tasted defeat for two years. In addition, Lincoln had started to become the commander and run the war from his office in Washington. He was concerned about results and elections, and he came to feel that he was the most qualified to manage and direct the war. In 1862 this caused the alignment of Grant and

Lincoln - two men who certainly had been associated with the agony of defeat in their careers. This union turned out to be a good marriage.

As General George B. McClellan's loyalty was being questioned, an interesting development was taking place. Perhaps the most revealing remark Lincoln ever made about his relationship with McClellan was concerning an entirely different general.

Earlier in 1863, Grant fought the battle of Shiloh inexpertly, suffering a shameful surprise and losing many men who need not have been lost. There was great clamour against him; he was denounced as an incompetent and drunkard, and tremendous political pressure was put on Lincoln to remove him.

A.K. McClure, the Pennsylvania politician who was intimate with the President, was convinced that Lincoln, as a matter of general politics, could not sustain himself if he attempted to retain Grant. Late one night, he went to the White House to argue the point and told Lincoln, *"with all the earnestness I could command,"* that he simply must get rid of General Grant.

Then, as McClure described it, *"Lincoln remained silent for what seemed a very long time. He then gathered himself up in his chair and said in a tone of earnestness that I shall never forget : I can't spare this man; he fights!"*

Are we to believe that Grant was the only capable general remaining in the Union who would fight? Then why did Grant go west and command, for an additional two years, with only limited success, against the lesser Southern troops and generals? If the President's convictions really backed up his word, then Grant would have been given greater responsibility in the Eastern theatre of combat. To the betterment of the Union, Grant went West and grew in favor with the President. Grant in the Western field, never asked the President for a thing. This fact further pleased Lincoln. It is important to understand that Lincoln and Grant had forged a pact that would last until the end of the conflict.

Chapter 3

Meade was born in 1815, of American parents, in Cadiz, Spain. He could trace his roots to men and women of great integrity, religious conviction, and business ability. His great grandfather from Philadelphia, a strong supporter of General George Washington, was known as "Honest" George Meade. Richard Worsham Meade, his father, developed a remarkable talent in the import/export business at an early age. While in Spain in 1804, his grandfather, George began to experience a decline in health and died in 1808. General Meade's grandmother, a fine woman of education and breeding with strong religious convictions, was a devoted wife and an affectionate mother. Although the family fortune was gone, she carried on and kept the traditions of the Meade family alive.

George Meade's father carried on the Meade tradition in business, and by hard work and numerous dealings became a very wealthy man. However, Spain was economically unstable, so a majority of the elder Meade's claims were not paid. Finally, through the Treaty of Florida in 1819, a pact between the United States and Spain, all outstanding claims were assumed by the United States government. This encouraged Richard Meade and gave him hope that these claims would finally be settled. This necessitated the Meades' departure from Cadiz, Spain, and their return to Philadelphia, Pennsylvania.

The family now consisted of ten children. George Gordon was the eighth child and second son. He was educated in good private schools and had an ambition to enter law. However, his father, having moved the family to Washington, D.C., continued to press his claims to no avail. This bitter and constant disappointment climaxed in his death at the early age of fifty.

His hope for a law career now dashed, George Gordon sought an appointment to West Point. His older brother, Richard, was appointed a midshipman to the Naval Academy in 1826.

After failing in his application, Meade was accepted into West Point in the summer of 1831 on an appointment by President Andrew Johnson. Meade was fifteen years and eight months of age. He had little trouble with the curriculum at West Point and was well liked. He graduated on July 1, 1835, ranking nineteenth in his class of fifty-six.

Meade married Margaretta Sergeant, daughter of the Honorable John Sergeant, a distinguished member of Congress, lawyer of Constitutional law and vice-presidential nominee in 1832 on Henry Clay's presidential ticket. The marriage took place on December 31, 1840, in Philadelphia, at the residence of the bride's parents. The couple had six children: two daughters, Henrietta and Sarah, and sons John Sergeant, George III, Willie and Spencer.

Shortly after his marriage, Meade reentered the army, and on May 1842 was assigned to the Topographical Engineers. He was briefly stationed in Philadelphia when orders came to report to Texas by August 12, 1845, to serve in the Army of Observation under Brigadier General Zachary Taylor. Trouble with Mexico was always a possibility on the Southern border.

Meade left his wife and three children, one of whom was seriously ill, and at age thirty departed for the next step in his career. His wife was supportive of his Army career. Meade, now a lieutenant, continued to gain the esteem of those with whom he came in contact.

Meade served ably during the Mexican War under Taylor. His efficiency elevated the Bureau of Topographical Engineers to a prominent facet of the U.S. Army. Meade was promoted to First Lieutenant on August 4, 1851.

During the early fifties, Meade became involved in the construction of the lighthouses in Florida, namely Sandy Key, Carysfort Reef, Cape Hatteras, and Key West Harbor. His usefulness in this capacity and his direct dealing with the Secretary of State, Secretary of War, and the Chairman of the Lighthouse Board, who held him in high regard, provided that any thought of transferring Meade elsewhere was dismissed. On May 31, 1856, Meade turned over his command to Colonel W.F. Reynolds. Meade's work in the field of lighthouses showed time and time again his admirable skills of investigation and careful statement. This type of precise action was an outgrowth of Meade's scrupulous truthfulness. Integrity pervaded everything he did and said in his daily life.

On April 24, 1856, Meade was promoted to Captain and on May 20, 1857, assigned to duty in charge of the lake survey. When these surveys were started in 1841, the lake region was sparsely populated, but by 1856 settlers began pouring in and commerce was steadily increasing along the lake's ports.

Meade's principal accomplishment from 1857 to 1861 was the survey of Lake Huron and the completion of the Saginaw Bay Project. Meade made advances in the American method which is the determination of longitudes by electric telegraph. Toward the end of his duty, secession of the Southern states loomed on the horizon.

Meade certainly was no politician, however, he loved his country and he trusted the citizens to do the right thing. Times were difficult for military men. Those who felt an allegiance to the Southern cause began resigning their commissions. Many who were comrades-in-arms during the Mexican War now departed to their own cause. Meade, from the outset, determined where his allegiance would be counted. He strongly denounced the Southern leadership for urging and goading their people in the wrong direction. He never knew that use of force was not the solution. A patriot, he would give his total energy and knowledge as a soldier to the salvation of his country.

Early on, two things were abundantly clear to Meade. First, if the political agitation continued as it was, then the ultimate answer would be civil war. Meade knew the North and South equally well, having spent many years in each sector of the nation. Secondly, he knew the North had an immense superiority over the South in terms of manpower and resources. The ultimate winner would be the North.

Because of the resignation of Southern officers in Detroit, Meade could see and feel the distrust people had for the military. The citizens of Detroit wanted all military officers to assemble at a public meeting to take an oath of allegiance to the United States. The officers met at Meade's office and all but one declined. They felt it was unbecoming for an officer to be at such a meeting, that it would be a dangerous precedent to take this oath on demand and in the presence of a crowd. They concluded that the organizers of the meeting were unjustified in calling it. They did, however, create and sign a document that was forwarded to the War Department, showing their eagerness and willingness to take an oath of allegiance whenever called upon by the War Department.

Chapter 4

Soon after the firing on Ft. Sumter, North Carolina, Meade made repeated and urgent requests to the army for active duty. Hearing no response, he went to Washington and protested in June of 1861. Nothing was done and he returned to Detroit.

It was later determined that the long delay was caused by the disinclination to confer higher rank upon him. In addition, the department was reluctant to allow regular army officers to accept positions in the voluntary service. Meade was prepared to do so. It would pave the way for him to

accept the colonelcy of a Michigan regiment of volunteers offered by Governor Austin Blair. However, much to his surprise, on August 31, 1861, Meade was notified of his appointment as

Brigadier General of Volunteers and told to report to Washington and General George B. McClellan.

He was assigned to the Pennsylvania Reserves commanded by General George McCall, and given command of the Second Brigade. This group was formed by a special act of the legislature and passed at the insistence of Pennsylvania's Governor Andrew C. Curtain. Shortly thereafter, the Union was defeated at Bull Run and the Pennsylvania Reserves were integrated into the Army of the Potomac.

Meade, now forty-six, was to embark on another facet of his career: a field of labor entirely different from that which he had pursued during the past thirteen years. Ahead was the clamor of camp life, the long tough marches, and the horrors of war. The scientific exploration part of Meade's career was over. There were those who said his scientific mind should not be wasted to become mere food for powder. But there was no choice. The General was well aware where honor and duty lay. His loving wife concurred and did all in her power to support her husband.

Nothing could give a better idea of the sentiments by which Meade was inspired at this momentous period in his country's history than the words which he addressed to a close friend in a letter written a few days before he took the field. Meade wrote: *"I cordially agree with you, in earnest prayers that a merciful Providence would so guide the hearts of the rulers on both sides as to terminate this unnatural contest. But, as for myself, I have ever held it to be my duty to uphold and maintain the Constitution and resist the disruption of the government. With this opinion, I hold the other side responsible for the existing condition of affairs. Besides as a soldier, holding a mission, it has always been my judgement that duty required I should disregard all political questions, and obey orders. I go into the field with these principles, trusting to God to dispose of my life and actions in accordance with my daily prayer, that His will and not mine be done."*

While in the field and away from home, Meade corresponded regularly with his wife and family. His letters give additional insight into his character. From Camp Pierpont, Virginia, on November 14, 1861, Meade wrote to his son, John Sergeant Meade, about "Baldy" - the General's horse. *"I would like very much to have a really fine horse, but it costs so much I must try to get along with my old hacks."* Baldy remained with Meade in the field until the spring of 1864. During that time, Baldy and the general became close friends. Baldy was wounded twice under Meade at the Battle of Bull Run, shot through the neck at Antietam, wounded at Fredericksburg, and again at Gettysburg. At Antietam, the ball remained in his body. In the spring of 1864, Meade, fearing that he might become an embarrassment in the campaign which was about to commence, sent him to pasture near Philadelphia, where he outlived his master.

As was his custom when corresponding with his wife, The General wrote straight to the point and did not mince his words. On November 17, 1861, Meade stated, *"People who think the war is about to close, because we have achieved a signal success (Navy at Port Royal) are very short sighted."*

On November 24, 1861, Meade told her, in talking about the recruits they were training, *"We have been weeding out some of the worst, but owing to the vicious system of electing successors which prevails, those who take their place are no better. I ought not perhaps to write to you, and* you must understand it is in confidence, but you asked me to tell you everything freely and without disguise, and I have complied with your request."

On December 31, 1861, from Camp Pierpont, Meade writes to his wife, "Do you know today is our wedding day and my birthday? Twenty-one years ago we pledged our faith to each other, and I doubt if any other couple live who, with all the ups and downs of life, have had more happiness with each other than you and I. I trust a merciful Providence will spare us both to celebrate yet many returns of the day, and that we shall see our children advancing in life prosperously and happily."

The war finally became a reality to Meade and his troops in the battle of Gaine's Mill. During this seven days of battle June 26 to July 1, the total loss in McClellan's army was 15,249 killed, wounded, or captured.

Even though wounded, Meade continued to lead his charges until he finally was overcome by loss of blood. The time was 7:00 p.m., June 30, 1862. Meade stated that his injuries were not dangerous, but many thought that they were looking upon him for the last time. He arrived home in Philadelphia on July 4.

During his recovery, Meade remained quiet and with his family and close friends. As he progressed, he was eager to return to the field and his command. Despite the advice of his physician, Meade once again said goodbye to his loving wife and family and set out for the field on August 11. The General was absent for exactly forty-two days.

On August 18, 1862, writing from Fredericksburg, Meade stated, *"I visited my old regiments and was received with much enthusiasm, and I really believe the whole command, officers and men, were sincerely glad to see me back."*

Chapter 5

After conversing with numerous officers, Meade concluded that his Pennsylvania Reserves truly saved the army. Without the strategic change of base, which kept the enemy in check on June 30, the Army of the Potomac undoubtedly would have split their forces in two, each of which then could have been destroyed. The Second Battle of Bull Run, August 28-30 was fought with 14,462 Federal soldiers killed, wounded, or missing. Meade survived the fighting and although Baldy was hit in the leg, he was not badly hurt.

On September 18, 1862, in the battle near Sharpsburg, Meade wrote the following to his wife:

"I commanded the division of Pennsylvania Reserves in the action at South Mountain Gap on the 14th. Our division turned the enemy's left flank

and gained the day. Their movements were the admiration of the whole army, and I gained great credit. I was not touched or my horse. Yesterday and the day before my division commenced the battle and was in the thickest of it. I was hit by a spent grape shot, giving me a severe contusion in the right thigh. Baldy was shot in the neck, but will get over it. When General Hooker was wounded, General McClellan placed me in command of the Army Corps, over General Rickett's head, who out ranks me. This selection is a great compliment, and answers all my wishes in regard to my desire to have my services appreciated. I cannot ask for more, and am grateful for the merciful manner I have been protected, and for the good fortune that has attended me. I go into action today as the Commander of an Army Corps. If I survive, my two stars are secure, and if I fall, you will have my reputation to live on."

During the Battle of Antietam, 12,410 Union troops were killed, wounded, or lost. Because many were volunteers, they wandered off when the wounded left the battle field. They consisted of cowards, men who left the battleground with the wounded, and did not return for days, plus stragglers, and the skulkers. Meade said that this was common for both sides but the ratio was particularly high for the Union's all-volunteer army.

At this time there was great political jockeying for rank and command. Hooker was in the field with only the command of corps under Burnside. Reynolds would command Meade's former corps while Meade continued the command of his division. Meade, as always, was thankful for his command. Inwardly he was disappointed by the interference of the politicians and the petty bickering among military men. Once again he felt Providence had passed him by. But life and war went on, and Meade continued to pour his intelligence, energy, and leadership into the remainder of this senseless conflict.

In December of 1862 at the battle of Fredericksburg, another 12,653 Union soldiers were killed, wounded, or lost. Meade wrote to his wife concerning the battle: *"I was myself unhurt, although a ball passed through my hat, so close, that if it had come from the front instead of the side, I would have been a goner."*

As the winter moved on and a new year was born, the political overtone in this Civil War made itself felt more and more. Burnside was being tied up in Washington by the President, Edwin M. Stanton, Secretary of War, and Major General Henry W. Halleck. His generals Sumner, William B. Franklin, and Hooker were restive. Those in command were not allowed to command. Their hands were tied and the Union forces again ground to a standstill. Meade let his opinion be known among the officers at this time, saying risks must be taken if the Union's cause is to advance and succeed. The army could not wait until all the elements were perfect, or the enemy would again attack and foil Union plans. Meade was given command of the Fifth Corps.

By the end of January, Burnside was relieved of duty as Commander of the Army of the Potomac. Sumner and Franklin were both relieved from duty and ordered to report to Washington. Meade characterized Burnside as a man with determination and nerve, but lacking judgement, knowledge, and deficient in mental capacity to be a successful commander. Meade felt Burnside was in a weakened position among the officers and men who knew he was not comfortable with command. Hooker was a good soldier, Meade said, but he aligned himself with those that tended to have a bad influence on his conduct. Meade concluded that time alone would determine if his analysis of Hooker was correct.

As January passed into February, the weather took command of the course of events. Rain, mud, and more mud brought all events in the military to a standstill. Meade related to his wife that there was word the personnel in the Provost Marshall domain in Washington were making a common practice of reading letters to and from the officer corps. Meade stated that he failed to see how this could have been true. He told his wife in a letter that he would never believe this, *"but I maintain no government in the world would take advantage of such confidential intercourse to find a man guilty, and I don't believe any of my letters have ever been opened."*

Time moved slowly and Meade, like many others, must have been disappointed with the inactivity of the Army of the Potomac. Meade wrote: *"I am completely fuddled about politics, and am afraid the people are very much demoralized. I trust one thing or another will be done. Either carry on the war as it ought to be, with overwhelming means, both material and personnel, or else give it up altogether. I am tired of half-way measures and efforts, and of the indecisive character of operations up to this time. I don't know whether these sentiments will be considered disloyal, but they are certainly mine; with the understanding, however, that I am in favor of the first, namely, a vigorous prosecution of the war with all the means in our power."*

The old reserves that Meade had led with distinction had subscribed fifteen hundred dollars to present him with a new sword, sash, belt, etc., around the end of the month of April. As usual, the General preferred to be of no part of this ceremony, because he was a man of humble nature. Meade told many he would rather they gave the money to the wives and families of those who had been lost in the war. He felt uncomfortable having this bestowed upon him.

After the battle at Chancellorsville, May 3-5 where Meade's men performed well before a retreat was called, Union losses amounted to 12,145 killed, wounded, and missing. Meade was flattered by the positive comments made by fellow officers concerning his ability. Meade said Hooker, after retreating, sadly said he should turn the army over to Meade. Hooker apparently felt he had gone the limit and enough was enough. However, Hooker's one great advantage over his predecessors was that there was no "cut-throat" action by his subordinate generals to replace him.

After the blunders and retreat at Chancellorsville, there were those who felt that Hooker would succumb to the "new general of the next battle" syndrome that had gripped the throat of the Union decision makers. In writing to his wife from Falmouth, Virginia on May 23, 1863, Meade made these comments: *"It is understood that the cabinet is divided, Salmon P. Chase upholding Hooker, Montgomery Blair and William H. Seward in opposition. I have always thought Hooker would be allowed another chance, and I sincerely hope and trust and indeed believe, he will do better, as I think he now sees the policy of caution is not a good one. Until our recent imbroglio, he has always spoken of me very warmly, though he has never asked for my advice, or listened to my suggestions. What he is going to do or say I don't know, but I shall not count on any friendly offices from him. Still I should be sorry to see him removed, unless a*

41

decidedly better man is substituted."

There was very little activity in mid-June. Rumor was widespread that Lee would move his army into Maryland before meeting the Army of the Potomac again. Meade felt that this strategy was ill-advised because such a move would arouse the North and allow it to awaken from the lethargic state in which it had been. The administration would immediately call for more troops to replace those who were leaving the ranks, their duty time having been served. No word came from Hooker, who maintained his normal employment of orders. His habit was to keep his commands and their commanders, "in the dark" until the last minute.

Meade's wife, once again had made known her feelings that he should be placed in command of the Army of the Potomac, and that she was troubled because he had not been so elevated. Meade answered her concerns as he wrote to her:

" I thought that had all blown over, and I think it has, except in your imagination, and that of some others of my kind friends . . . I have not the vanity to think my capacity so pre-eminent, and I know there are plenty of others equally competent with myself though their names may not have been

so much mentioned for these reasons. I have never indulged in any dreams of ambition, contented to await events, and do my duty in the sphere it pleases God to place me in, and I really think it would be as well for you to take the same philosophical view; but do you know, I think your ambition is being aroused and that you are beginning to be bitten with the dazzling prospect of having for a husband a Commanding General of any army. How is this? "

The closeness between Meade and his wife is evident in this letter as Meade kidded his beloved mate because she not only loved him, but felt that he was capable of greater things.

On June 30, 1863, Meade would celebrate the first anniversary of his wounds in the Seven Days Battle - wounds so severe that most felt their leader would leave the field for the final time.

On the morning of June 26, Meade, under orders, began to move his corps to a place called Frederick City, Maryland. On the 27th, they arrived at Ballenger Creek, just outside of Frederick City where the encampment of the corps was to take place. Immediately, Meade went into the city, hoping to meet with Hooker, whom he had not seen for two weeks, and gain some information as to new orders and the whereabouts of Lee's army. Since the General had not arrived, Meade returned to camp empty-handed.

At 4:00 a.m. the following morning, June 28th, Meade was awakened by a voice asking for him. The voice was that of Colonel James A. Hardie of General Henry W. Halleck's staff who was bearing important dispatches from the General. The transfer of command was short and simple. Meade was now Commander of the Army of the Potomac. As was Meade's custom, he immediately began to "dig-in" and place his full energy and attention to the task at hand. The magnitude of this undertaking was unfathomable. This critical change of commanders was made when the army was in full movement with troops dispersed over a great area of land trying to track down the finest army that the world had ever seen, which was led by the ablest general at the disposal of the enemy.

The high officers of the Army of the Potomac, having served with Meade during battle, were well aware of his strict attention to duty, his constant presence with his command, his quick perception, the generous support he gave at all times to his superior officers and his promptness and action in decision.

Having completed his plans on June 28, 1863, Meade set the Army of the Potomac in motion. By the afternoon of June 30th, the army completed two hard marches. The weather had been intensely hot. The roads were not only poor, but stifling from the dust except when relief came from a scattered drizzle and plagued the Union forces. Meade feared the breakdown of his troops if he pushed them harder. However, it was the forced marches that Meade ordered that led to the concentration of the Army of Northern Virginia by Lee in and around Gettysburg.

Without waiting, Meade, while his army was on the march, sent out engineers to find a suitable ground to wage the impending battle. The Army of the Potomac was on the move and morale was uplifted because the men knew their commander was making decisions, taking necessary chances, and looking to meet the enemy in battle. Perhaps most importantly, Meade's top officers, Reynolds, Winfield S. Hancock, Gouverneur K. Warren, Andrew A. Humphreys, and John Sedgwick, were completely briefed and had discussed the

Commanding General's intentions for the army and the actions to be employed.

On the morning of June 30, 1863, the exact location and the intention of the Southern forces was still unknown to Meade. " *About half-past eleven o'clock Meade received the first positive intelligence of the movement of the enemy on Gettysburg, and of the engagement of his advance at that place. It was brought to him by an aid-de-camp of Reynolds, Captain Stephen N. Weed, who left his gallant chief at ten o'clock outside of Gettysburg and who had ridden hard with his message. Captain Weed reported that General Reynolds had said to him, 'Ride at your utmost speed to General Meade. Tell him the enemy is advancing in strong force, and that I fear they will get to the heights beyond the town before I can. I will fight them inch by inch, and if driven back into town, I will barricade the streets and hold them back as long as possible. Don't spare your horse - never mind if you kill him'.*

General Meade seemed disturbed at first by this news, lest he should lose the position referred to at Gettysburg. At his request, the officer repeated the message, then he seemed reassured, and said:

'Good! That is just like Reynolds; he will hold on to the bitter end'."

At 4 p.m., under orders from General Meade, Hancock arrived on the field at or near the cemetery. Taking charge and regrouping the retreating Union forces was Hancock's main priority. In these efforts he was aided by Generals Buford, Howard and Warren in directing stragglers and the formation of a solid line. At approximately 6:00 p.m., General Slocum, the most senior of officers, arrived on the field and Hancock turned over his command and left immediately for Taneytown, Maryland to confer with Meade. At the same time of 4:00 p.m., Lee approached the town and before dark, two-thirds of the army was consolidated. Thus the Southern army converged upon Gettysburg from the north and the Northern troops approached Gettysburg from the south.

Chapter 6

When Meade was appointed Commander-in-Chief of the Army of the Potomac on June 28, 1863, what he didn't know was that he was the third choice of Lincoln and Stanton. Enter General Henry W. Halleck, aide to the President and Commander-in Chief of all military forces for the Union. He was a passive player during the course of the war. His duties were confined to passing along instructions from Lincoln and reminding the appropriate commanders to keep the army between the enemy forces and Washington at all times. On his behalf, Halleck was a very able organizer. However, as a leader of armies, he was truly incompetent. In 1862, he had been ordered to Washington where he put his abilities to work for the North, but his lack of strategic sense handicapped the commanders in the field. Halleck's deficiency may have convinced the President he was a master strategist in his own right. It should be noted that Halleck's input concerning a new Commander for the Army of the Potomac was not sought and Lincoln and Stanton proceeded with the selection process.

Initially, General Darius Couch was offered the appointment of the Commander of the Army of the Potomac. Stationed at Harrisburg, Pennsylvania, Couch was recognized as a fine soldier and career officer. He was in his present assignment because he submitted to the commands of Hooker. However, due to his poor health, Couch was unable to accept the promotion. Couch offered his highest recommendation to two most able officers. They were Reynolds and Meade. One would feel that the recommendation of these two men, both natives of Pennsylvania, was not by mere coincidence. Upon hearing that he was going to receive consideration from Washington, Reynolds immediately left for that city and a consultation with the President. A truly fine officer, Reynolds was considered a soldier's general. At this time and by this action, the political situation was brought into true light and focus.

Reynolds stated that he would not accept the command unless all ties between the military and Washington would be severed immediately. He felt the field commander needed the freedom to run his own battle without daily orders from the Capitol. The reply received was expected and obvious and Reynolds had no recourse but to decline the offer.

It is reported that Lincoln then concluded that Meade would do. Unaware that Meade was a Pennsylvanian, Lincoln, when informed of this fact by Stanton, remarked, "And will fight well on his own dunghill." A strong vote of confidence was not being offered to Meade, like the school superintendent confirmed on an 5-4 vote. Regardless of what action one undertakes , it will never be enough to satisfy the board. Had Meade been aware of the on-going events, he probably would have declined the offer. However, Meade entered his tent office and wrote, in pencil, this brief acceptance to Halleck in Washington.

"The order to place me in command of this army is received. As a soldier I obey it and to the utmost of my ability will execute it. Totally unexpected as it has been, and , in ignorance of

the exact conditions of the troops and position of the enemy, I can only now say that it appears to me I must move forward toward the Susquehanna, keeping Washington and Baltimore well covered. If the enemy is checked in his attempt to cross, or if he turns toward Baltimore, (I intend) to give him battle. I would say that I trust every available man that can be spared will be sent to me, as from all accounts, the enemy is in strong force. So soon as I can post myself up, I will communicate more in detail."

This clear statement was eagerly awaited by the Washingtonians. Knowing Meade to be energetic, courageous, and a dutiful officer whose troops were among the best in the Army, the President was overjoyed. He knew that Meade was not political and that he would adopt a subordinate role.

General Meade wrote to his wife: *"At the White House, he was heard to remark as if to himself, 'I tell you I think a great deal of that fine fellow Meade'."*

Thus humbling himself before Almighty God, the sober and scholarly Meade led his hosts into battle. Fortunately for Meade and the Union, the events through July 3 transpired so rapidly that time would not permit any direct interference from Washington. It became evident Meade was the right man at the right time.

On June 28, 1863, Meade, from his new headquarters for the Army of the Potomac, wrote the following to the nation. These are the words of a humble servant preparing to accomplish that which must be done for the common good.

"By direction of the President of the United States, I hereby assume command of the Army of the Potomac. As a soldier, in obeying this order

- an order totally unexpected and unsolicited - I have no promises or pledges to make. The country looks to this army to relieve it from the destruction and disgrace of a hostile invasion. Whatever fatigues and sacrifices we may be called upon to undergo, let us have in view constantly the magnitude of the interest involved, and let every man determine to do his duty, leaving to an all-controlling Providence the decision of the contest. It is with just diffidence that I relieve in the command of this army, an eminent and accomplished soldier, whose name must ever appear conspicuous in the history of its achievements; and I rely upon the hearty support

of my companions in arms to assist me in the discharge of the duties of the important trust which has been confided to me."

George Gordon Meade
Major-General Commanding

Chapter 7

Oh, Gettysburg! Why, Gettysburg? No one can answer for sure. However, the town has many interesting features - none greater than the geographical location. Like the hub of a great wheel, the spokes of roads go forth to various points of strategic importance. Due west 25 miles is Chambersburg, county seat of Franklin County, the only community north of the Mason Dixon Line to be destroyed by fire in 1864 by the Rebel forces.

Due east 24 miles is the city of York. Northwest, Carlisle is 28 miles away and 19 miles further north is the capital city, Harrisburg. Thirty-two miles to the southwest is Frederick, Maryland. South, southwest 12 miles, you will find the community of Emmitsburg, Maryland. Hanover, Pennsylvania is south, southeast of Gettysburg 14 miles.

It is interesting to note that the railroad came to Gettysburg from Hanover and then it came to an end. The railroad played a vital role during the first day of the battle. The road system was ideal for troop and supply movement. This aspect may have been a contributing factor - the armies tended to congregate at the hub of the wheel. Historians have agreed that the intention to do battle around Gettysburg was neither the brainstorm of Meade nor Lee.

It was known as the great Civil War, and a small part of it was this battle fought around a small farming town in southcentral Pennsylvania called Gettysburg. This epic struggle forged, from a land divided, the beginning of a greater nation. Two armies fought here, each of which believed to the utmost the cause for which they so notably aspired. These young men, hardly soldiers, possessed little training and fewer military skills, but embodied a sincere commitment to their causes and the courage of their convictions, which made them unique in the annals of warfare. There were no long-range guns, no tanks or air support, nor even acceptable communications by modern standards. And yet, in their glorious lines, crouched behind a stone wall or eyeball to eyeball, they came to this place that their cause might be triumphant. It was truly a noble struggle waged around this quiet little town on July 1, 2, and 3, 1863.

Today, over one hundred and fifty years later, the town is still small and beautiful and the orchards that make Adams County unique still dominate the surrounding countryside. Yes, the seminary (1821) that gave its name to that famous ridge so long ago is still about the business of preparing young men and women for a life in the ministry. Pennsylvania College (1832) has likewise stood the test of time and has developed into a fine college of liberal arts. And yet, as one visits "The Field," the courage and glory , sorrow and suffering, and the colossal events that evolved on this compact piece of land truly allow the windmills of our mind to generate a sense of what THEY DID HERE!

If we try hard enough, we may be able to see Michael Jacobs, professor at Pennsylvania College, or his student son Henry, as they peered through the garret window of their Gettysburg residence through the eyes of the telescope equipped with a fine four-inch Vienna lens. These men were not only eyewitnesses, but immediately after the battle became chroniclers also. They did extensive research and collected data from other witnesses and participants alike.

The father, Michael Jacobs, published his manuscript in November, 1863, and titled his work, _Notes of the Rebel Invasion of Maryland and Pennsylvania and the Battle of Gettysburg_. This book was one of the first accounts of the battle. Many events were observed from his garret window in a 2 1/2 story brick residence that still stands on the northwest corner of Middle and Washington streets.

Finally on Friday, July 3, 1863, there was a calm, but it was not destined to last. In the afternoon the shot of a signal gun sounded, and the artillery of both sides responded. Henry E. Jacobs vividly recalls the scene in his book, _Notes on the Life of a Churchman:_

"One hundred and fifty guns thundering at once. The earth racked, above the tumult, one gun on Cemetery Hill was heard like an instrument carrying the air, while the rest accompanied it. The earth shook violently when it sounded. A house *near us was struck. Then there came the longing and the stillness of the silence. Was this the calm before the storm? Sensing the changing mood from the depths of the cellar, the older Jacobs could no longer contain his curiosity. Henry wrote, My father cannot be induced to remain with us. He felt by intuition what was coming. He has the glass with him in the garret. There he saw the line of Pickett forming on Seminary Ridge in magnificent array. Then comes the roar of the artillery and the crash of smaller arms. The din is resumed, only the tone is not so loud. It is not long. He sees them going back, no longer in serried ranks, but as individuals, broken, creeping through the wrecked corn field, a handful compared to those who had sallied forth. It is too much for him to remain longer alone. He calls: Henry, Henry, come at once. Here is a scene you will never have the opportunity again to see in your life. It is worth all the risk. Do not miss it! I went there and I could see clearly the stragglers working their way back to the Confederate line."*

Chapter 8

The battles of Fredericksburg and Chancellorsville were just concluded and once again the Southern forces claimed them as victories. In fact, Lee and his veteran troops were on a significant run of success: a run so compelling that Lee devised his plan to move north and to carry the fight to the Union on their home ground.

Victory and success created a positive atmosphere for the Southern cause. New volunteers were quickly accepted into the ranks. The feeling of being near the action and sharing in the glory was in the mind and heart of the rebel men. The Army of Northern Virginia was truly on a high note and their songs boasted of ending this war in victory.

Lee now considered the possibility of invading

the North. However, important factors had to be discussed and analyzed before an invasion could begin. The extremely high morale that prevailed among the Southern troops at this time had its down-side. First, the ugly head of overconfidence appeared. Second, the utter contempt that the South felt for the Northern troops would not serve them well in the long run. Third, Lee himself believed his troops were invincible - was he asking them to try to accomplish the impossible?

On May 15, 1863, Lee went to Richmond to meet with President Jefferson Davis and Secretary of War, James Seddon. Many proposals were discussed by other generals; however, Lee completely overwhelmed the others with his brilliant strategy. Lee was convinced that he needed to go on the offensive. He trusted that this maneuver would keep his capital from immediate attack. This was a huge risk because Richmond would be left basically unprotected. Lee also felt that Grant might be pulled away from Vicksburg in order to bolster the Eastern campaign. Lee's ambitious plan allowed him to hope for a decisive victory over Hooker. After all, he felt, the time was ripe to draw the Union out into the open and inflict a decisive blow for the South. Furthermore, it was no secret that England, Russia , and France were showing favorable signs toward the South. If Lee was to establish his army in the North, he felt that England would immediately recognize Southern independence. Lee felt he would be able to secure supplies - and possibly even recruits - north of the Mason Dixon line. With foreign intervention and armed support, the North might seek peace. Plus, the capture of cities like Washington, Philadelphia, and possibly New York, seemed realistic goals. Davis felt that success was within their grasp. The time and factors were right.

Big city folks had kept the war at arms length since it did not enter the North or their neighborhood. Lincoln and his advisors were having a most difficult time securing a competent General for the Army of the Potomac. Lincoln's decisions met time and time again with failure. It would have been reasonable to assume that after the Union defeat at Chancellorsville, Lincoln would have relieved his commander immediately. However, he waited and played a baiting game to produce the right set of circumstances that would convince Hooker to ask to be relieved of his command.

Meade was awakened from his sleep and presented the command of the Army of the Potomac. The time was afternoon, June 28, 1863.

Meade went to confer with Hooker. Meade said later while testifying before the committee on the conduct of the war: *"My predecessor, General Hooker, left the camp in a very few hours after I relieved him. I received from him to intimation of any plan, or any views that he may have had upon to that moment, and am not aware that he had any, but was waiting for the exigencies of the occasion to govern him, just as I had to do subsequently."* It was growing late in the day and Meade was thrown entirely upon his own resources.

Suppose you could have been there. What would be your initial move as Commander? Meade's first act was to appoint Kilpatrick to the Division of the Cavalry under General Hugh E. Stahl and immediately promote George A. Custer, 5th U.S. Cavalry, Wesley Merritt, 2nd U.S. Cavalry, and Elon J. Farnsworth, 8th Illinois Cavalry. These exceptional young captains were elevated by Meade to the rank of Brigadier General. This change was completed in record time by Halleck, or Meade simply went ahead without official permission. Meade's aggressive movement was designed to improve efficiency in the Union's Cavalry. He would be rewarded on the final day of the encounter. Meade's second act was an important decision concerning General Henry J. Hunt. Under Hooker, Hunt's role had been diminished to a staff position at headquarters. Meade's direction placed all decisions concerning artillery under Hunt's control and command. He would make the decisions as to where, when, and how much artillery would be in what section of the field, and for what period of time. The day of generals controlling their own artillery and creating chaos were past. Hunt now exercised artillery authority and the batteries' central coordination. This man's gifted ability would be evidenced, especially during the three-day battle around Gettysburg.

The makeup of the opposing armies is truly a study in opposites. With the demise of General Stonewall Jackson, Lee appointed Virginians to command positions. General Richard S. Ewell, 2nd Corps, Virginian, General Ambrose P. Hill, 3rd Corps, Virginian, and even General James "Pete" Longstreet, 1st Corps, although not born in the state, thought of himself as a Virginian. This principle can be found throughout the chain of command in the Army of Northern Virginia. The striking feature of the Southern military structure was the compact organization, ideal for dissemination of orders and communications. As has been pointed out, the Southern cause had been greatly bolstered by their recent deeds on the field of battle. They had established a mind-set that they truly were superior in combat and generalship and their successes were extolled and magnified.

In contrast, the Union had lost the equivalent of 58 regiments (58,000 men) since Chancellorsville. The organization of the Army of the Potomac was inferior to that of the South. The numerous corps and divisions weakened it: There were just too many commanders bogged down by massive staffs. The field artillery would have been vastly inferior if not for the self-sacrifice, courage, and intelligence of its officers and men. The Union had a smaller portion of army veterans. The army was not in favor with the War Department: It had rarely, if ever, had an official commendation after a success or sympathetic encouragement after a defeat. In addition, it may be safe to assume that the War

Department held a chronic terror for the safety of Washington. Therefore, a commander's orders concerning the safety of Washington subordinated his operations to those of the enemy.

At this time, the opposing camps were believed to be deployed as follows:

General Ewell's forces were positioned north, northwest of Gettysburg with the remainder at Fayetteville, Pennsylvania. The 3rd Corps were located at Cashtown and Greenwood, Pennsylvania. Longstreet's men were stationed at Chambersburg, Pennsylvania. The Southern Cavalry was at Hanover, Pennsylvania and Lee maintained his headquarters in Chambersburg, Pennsylvania.

The Union forces were located in the following towns:

1st Corps - South, southwest of Gettysburg at
        Marsh Run;
2nd Corps - Uniontown, Maryland
3rd Corps - Bridgeport, Maryland
5th Corps - Union Mills, Maryland
6th Corps - Manchester, Maryland
11th Corps - Emmitsburg, Maryland
12th Corps - Littlestown, Pennsylvania

Cavalry - under Brigadier General D.McGregg at
Manchester, Maryland;
- under Brigadier General Judson
Kilpatrick at Hanover, Pennsylvania
- under Buford near Gettysburg,
Pennsylvania

Meade's headquarters was located at Taneytown, Maryland.

One of the most exciting qualities of a great leader is the ability to delegate authority. This is keenly true during times of great stress and action. It is important to note that Meade exercised this privilege in relation to four men while at Gettysburg. The first was Buford. This man had revolutionized the tactics of the Union Calvary as evidenced during the conflicts at Brandy Station and Gettysburg. Buford, loyal to Meade, would be dead six months after the first day of July, 1863 falling victim to typhoid fever at the age of 37. However, on the initial day of the conflict, Buford had orders from Meade to go to Gettysburg to determine if the battle should be fought there. Buford encountered Lee's forces west of the town and the battle was engaged. Against great odds, Buford and his men were able to make a difference

- in fact, they held their ground and later allowed a retreat to Cemetery Hill, southwest of the town. This position, Buford contended would be ideal to accept the enemy.

The second man was Major General John Fulton Reynolds, from Lancaster, Pennsylvania, another trusted friend of Meade, who rallied his troops of the 1st Corps in support of Buford during the first day's action. Reynolds came into Gettysburg in reply to Buford's request for assistance. After surveying the field from the Seminary light tower and conferring with Buford, Reynolds immediately returned to his troops and entered the battle in the southwest sector. Great fighting raged at McPherson's Woods, where Reynolds was struck by a sharpshooters bullet and killed. His men continued the struggle without their fallen leader and against great odds.

Meade's third choice and Reynolds replacement was Major General Winfield Scott Hancock of Pennsylvania. Also loyal to Meade, Hancock was given express orders to pick the location to do battle, if, in fact, the battle should be waged around Gettysburg. Upon his arrival on the field, Hancock's presence rallied the troops, allowed them the time to reassemble, and thus prevented a chaotic ending to the Union's withdrawal to Cemetery Ridge. Once the Union line was intact, Hancock felt that this location would be ideal for the battle and reported that to Meade. Hancock suggested that Meade, when time permitted, come to Gettysburg for the final decision.

The fourth man was an engineer like the Commander, a close friend and respected soldier - Major General Gouveneur Kemble Warren. It is interesting to note that when Meade was told that he was the new Commander of the Army of the Potomac, and after conferring with the President's messenger, he went directly to the tent of his friend Warren. Upon arousing him from a deep sleep, Meade told him that he wanted Warren to become his Chief of Staff. The men talked briefly and Warren declined on the grounds that his engineering abilities could be put to good use in the field. He suggested that Butterfield, although an ally of Hooker, be retained, short term, because of his experience. Later Warren assisted in forming the Union line on Cemetery Ridge during the afternoon of the first day. During the second day, while on orders from Meade, Warren observed the exposure of the left flank of the entire Union forces at Little Round Top. By his prompt and expedient methods, fresh troops were rushed into the area and this vital position was secured.

To be able to delegate and have the confidence that matters were in excellent hands, allowed sufficient time for General Meade to map strategy, consolidate the Army, and prepare for the greatest battle that the American continent has ever known. This trust of men and teamwork were vital ingredients to the plan that would ultimately prevail.

It is important to note as preparations went forth, immediately prior to the battle around Gettysburg, York had surrendered to Rebel forces. The Southern flag also flew over the barracks at Carlisle. Ewell's men were poised to strike across the Susquehanna River at Harrisburg and also on the city of Philadelphia. Lee was within an eyelash of following Ewell. Without information from his Cavalry and Stuart, Lee could not wait a minute longer, but had to make a move. His proposed movement was abruptly halted when vital information was received from a Confederate spy. The spy - actor James Harrison - was under orders from Longstreet to bring vital information to him when possible. By secretly weaving a path through the Union lines, Harrison arrived at Longstreet's Chambersburg Headquarters on the evening of June 28th. He told Longstreet that the Federal troops were approaching the Mason Dixon line, north of Frederick, Maryland. Lee changed all orders upon receipt of this news. Ewell was told to move his scattered troops toward the main army. Early on July 1, these men were hurrying toward Gettysburg.

Chapter 9

At the start of the Southern invasion into Pennsylvania, the local citizens were very much concerned and worried. This concern was expressed in journals and local newspapers of the day. The journal of Dr. Philip Schaff illustrates their feelings as he wrote from his home in Mercersburg on June 18th, 1863:

"We are cut off from all mail communication and dependant on the flying and contradictory rumors of passengers, straggling soldiers, runaway Negroes, and spies. All the schools and stores were closed; goods are being hid or removed to the country, valuables buried in cellars or gardens and other places of concealment; the poor Negroes, the innocent cause of the war, are trembling like leaves and flying with their little bundles to the mountains,

especially the numerous run-away slaves from Virginia, from fear of being captured as 'contraband' and sold to the South; political passions run high; confidence is destroyed; innocent persons are seized as spies; the neighbor looks upon his neighbor with suspicion, and even sensible ladies have their imagination excited with pictures of horror far worse than death. This is the most tolerable state of things, and it would be a positive relief of the most painful suspended if the Rebel Army would march into town."

It is also interesting to note several accounts from Pennsylvania newspapers at this perilous time in the Commonwealth's history.

*"**Philadelphia**, June 15. A dispatch from Greencastle, Pennsylvania dated 10:30 a.m. reports that our troops were then passing there in retreat from Hagerstown, Maryland to Chambersburg.*

Hagerstown has been evacuated and all the stores and rolling stock of the railroad removed. Rumor fixes the Rebel force at ten thousand, which is probably an exaggeration."

*"**Harrisburg**, June 15, Governor Curtain has issued a proclamation stating that the President has called on Pennsylvania for fifty thousand men,*

to repel the invasion of the State and urge men to rush to arms to resist the advance of the Rebel troops now threatening our border."

"**Philadelphia**, June 16. The city is alive with excitement. The news of the Rebel advance has caused the most profound sensation. Intelligence is eagerly looked for from the interior. In view of the pressing emergency, Mayor Henry has issued the following proclamation:"

" Office of the Mayor
City of Philadelphia
12 o'clock noon, June 16

Citizens of Philadelphia:

In view of the urgent need for instant action to protect the Capitol of your state and secure the safety of our homes, I do hereby earnestly appeal to all citizens to close their places of business, and to connect themselves without delay with the existing military organization for the defense of the city.

Alex. Henry
Mayor of Philadelphia

To the People of Pennsylvania:

For nearly a week it has been publicly known that the Rebels were about to enter Pennsylvania.

On the 12th instant, an urgent call was made to the people to raise a Departmental Army Corps for the defense of the state. Yesterday, under the proclamation of the President, the Militia was called out.

Today a new and pressing exhortation has been given to furnish men. Philadelphia has not responded. Meanwhile the enemy is six miles this side of Chambersburg, and advancing rapidly.

Our Capital is threatened, and we may be disgraced by it's fall, while men who should be driving these outlaws from our soil are quibbling about the possible term of service for six months.

It was never intended to keep them beyond the continuance of the emergency. You all know this by what happened when the Militia was called out last autumn (Antietam Campaign). You then trusted the government and were not deceived. Trust it again now.

I will accept men without reference to the six months. If you do not wish to bear the ignominy of shirking from the defense of your State, come forward at once. Close your places of business and apply your hearts to the work. Come in such organizations as you can form.

General Couch has appointed Col. Ruff to superintend your organization. Report to him immediately."

There was excitement and fear in the air. All were apprehensive. The Governor had spoken: Pennsylvania had been invaded by a hostile Rebel force. The big question in the minds of the citizens was: *"Which way will the enemy move? Will he go West to the industrial complexes of the Commomwealth or will he turn East toward its political heart?"*

Who are the men in whom were entrusted the very survival of the Union? Surely, facing a general and his army who had not tasted defeat under his leadership would be next to a Herculean task. Could the North be expected to put up a major battle? They were farmers, mechanics, fishermen, laborers, professional and commercial men. They came to this crossroad town from their homes in

New York, Massachusetts, New Hampshire, Indiana, Michigan, Illinois, Minnesota, Vermont, Wisconsin, Ohio, Rhode Island, Connecticut, New Jersey, Maine, and Pennsylvania. To most it was the farthest point they had ever been from their homes. They came not knowing, they came to be soldiers, they came to save their country.

Yet this was the first and only major battle fought north of the Mason Dixon line. To many engaged here, this beautiful area was in their native state of Pennsylvania. Its leaders had an added incentive in this fight and they committed sixty-nine Infantry Regiments, ten Cavalry Regiments, and seven Batteries of Artillery for the battle around Gettysburg. The boys from Pennsylvania were as determined for victory as any group of men during the entire Civil War.

What was destined to make the battle special was the Union Commander. His presence can be captured in the words of Captain Joseph G. Rosengarten: *"General Meade, the commander on whom rested the responsibility, made the weightier by the unexpected order put him at the head of the Army of the Potomac, only three days before the battle which practically was the crisis of the war.*

His generalship was of the highest order, and his strategic and practical operations the best, yet, one other success has been too little regarded. His great moral and personal excellence was universally felt and recognized throughout the Army, and when he was put at it's head, that great body was at once lifted on a higher plane and became thoroughly inspired with a lofty purpose, and an earnest will to do all that should be asked. All joined in a silent mental revelation which permeates great masses of disciplined men, his fitness as a leader was universally recognized."

Meade - the scholar, the engineer, the Pennsylvanian, was the man who was destined to go after Lee's great Army at its zenith - an army with full knowledge that the South must win this important engagement for its very survival. The battle was transformed into a will of the mind and the gallantry of all the participants. The North and the Pennsylvanians perceived this struggle on their own hallowed ground, in the mindset to hold each flank at all costs, and to do whatever they must to save the day. It was a time when men rallied to the cause of duty with but one thought - to preserve the Union. These things were foremost in their minds and hearts. The time had come for a reversal of a trend. Lee's obsession that his command and his Army were superior to their foe must be quelled. Yet Meade had some ideas of his own. Quick decisions, adopting a strong and short battle line, and his faith in the ability of his officers and men would become allies to the Union Commander as the hot humid days and events of Wednesday, Thursday and Friday began to unfold.

In the midst of the impending encounter, with many strategic decisions to be made, Meade must have retired to the aide of the meeting room or under a nearby tree to write the following dispatch to all his commanders. The message is short, timely and precise. It addressed the aims of a man prepared to lead his charges against the finest army in the world:

Headquarters Army of the Potomac

June 30, 1863

"The Commanding General requests that previous to the engagement soon expected with the enemy, Corps and all other Commanding Officers will address their troops, explaining to them briefly the immense issues involved in the struggle. They are on our soil; the whole country looks anxiously to

this army to deliver it from the presence of the foe; our failure to do so will leave us no such welcome as the swelling millions of hearts with pride and joy at our success would give to every soldier of this army. Homes, firesides, and domestic alters, are involved. The army has fought well heretofore; it is believed it will fight more desperately and bravely than ever, if it is addressed in fitting terms. Corps and other Commanders are authorized to order the instant death of any soldier who fails in his duty this hour."

By command of:

Major General Meade

S. Williams, Assistant Adjutant-General"

General George G. Meade

Richard Worsam Meade - General Meade's father

Picture credit:
Civil War
Library and
Museum
1805 Pine St.
Philadelphia

Margaret Coates Butler - General Meade's mother

General John H. Reynolds fell at this point
on the 1st day of July;
his loss was mourned by all.

Lutheran Theological Seminary - 1862

Picture credit:U.S. Army History Institute, Carlisle Barracks

Lutheran Theological Seminary today
- notice Cupola used on July 1, by Buford and Reynolds,
and then the Southern Officers later in the same day -

Pennysylvania Monument
69 Infrantry Regiments - 9 Cavalry Regiments
7 Batteries of Artillery
Total present - 34,530
Killed or mortally wounded - 1182
Wounded - 3177
Missing 860

1st Pennsylvania Cavalry
1st Brigade - 2nd Division
Army of the Potomac

"FRIEND TO FRIEND"
Masonic Memorial

15,000 Masons fought at the Battle of Gettysburg
The monument depicts Capt. Henry H. Bingham (Union),
while wounded himself, coming to the aid of
Gen. Lewis A. Armistead (CSA), who fell wounded during
the rush over the Stone Wall during Pickett's Charge.
Armistead was a close friend to Gen. Whitfield S. Hancock,
who was also wounded at approximately the same time

Picture credit: Judy S. Walter 2013

Professor Michael Jacobs

Picture credit: Special Collection,
Musselman Library

*The residence of Professor Michael Jacobs, Instructor
at Pennsylvania College, and his son Henry.
- notice the Garret window -*

Henry E. Jacobs, son

Picture credit: Special Collection,
Musselman Library

"Old Baldy"
General Meade's faithful companion through
many difficult battles

Picture credit: U.S. Army History Institute, Carlisle Barracks

George Meade
The General's son and Aide

Picture credit: U.S. Army History Institute, Carlisle Barracks

Richard W. Meade, Captain U.S. Navy
The General's brother & Annapolis Graduate
Picture credit: U.S. Army History Institute, Carlisle Barracks

*Left to Right - Gouverneur K. Warren,
William H. French, General Meade, Henry J. Hunt,
Andrew A. Humphreys, and George Sykes*

Picture credit: U.S. Army History Institute, Carlisle Barracks

*General George Gordon Meade in 1866
at Boston, Massachusetts,
Meade's son is at his immediate right.*

Picture credit: U.S. Army History Institute, Carlisle Barracks

General Winfield Scott Hancock
2nd Corps

Picture credit: U.S. Army History Institute, Carlisle Barracks

General Lewis A. Armistead
1st Corps

General Robert E. Lee & Traveler

Picture credit: U.S. Army History Institute, Carlisle Barracks

James Longstreet "Old Pete"
Lt. General, 1st Corps

Picture credit: U.S. Army History Institute, Carlisle Barracks

Richard S. Ewell
Lt. General C.S.A.
2nd Corps

Picture credit: U.S. Army History Institute, Carlisle Barracks

Ambrose P. Hill
Lt. General C.S.A.
3rd Corps

Picture credit: U.S. Army History Institute, Carlisle Barracks

David McM. Gregg
Captain 6th U.S. Calvary

Picture credit: U.S. Army History Institute, Carlisle Barracks

Judson Kilpatrick
1st Lt. 1st U.S. Artillery
Picture credit: U.S. Army History Institute, Carlisle Barracks

General George A. Custer

Picture credit: U.S. Army History Institute, Carlisle Barracks,

General George G. Meade
Command of the Army of the Potomac
Portrait by celebrated 19th. Century Photographer,
Mathew Brady

General Meade's Headquarters, 1863
The Widow Leister's home

Picture credit: U.S. Army History Institute, Carlisle Barracks

All roads led to Gettysburg
(note road width and construction)

Picture credit: U.S. Army History Institute, Carlisle Barracks

Gettysburg 150 Years Later

*The Lutheran Seminary
is still standing
and now used as a museum
to honor the Civil War
and the heroes of that war*

Notice that same Cupola used on July 1, 1863

Picture credit: Penny Maxson 2013

Chapter 10

Let us pause for a moment and direct our attention to the area known and referred to as the "Pipe Creek." Meade's headquarters on June 30, 1863, was at Taneytown. Lee's army was forming under orders that no major engagement would begin until the army was totaly united. In contrast, the Union forces were scattered to the south and east of Gettysburg.

Meade had directed his chiefs of engineering artillery to also select a field of battle on which his army might be concentrated - whatever Lee's line of approach might be - whether by Gettysburg or Harrisburg. The terrain indicated the general line of Pipe Creek as a suitable location. Under existing circumstances on June 30, these views would have been wise and proper orders.

Prior to the great conflict at Gettysburg, Chambersburg held center stage for Lee and the Southern forces. It was here that strategies were planned and final decisions resolved.

On Tuesday, June 23rd, Jenkins Cavalry entered Chambersburg seeking and demanding provisions. The buildup continued as Ewell and a portion of his force set up headquarters in the Franklin Hotel on Memorial Square. Next came A. P. Hill and finally Lee, himself. The General came to town on Friday, June 26. Hill with his colorful plumed hat raised in the air, rose slowly to meet the General in center square. The two men exchanged greetings and rode a short distance from the staff to a short and private conversation. General Henry Heth's division of Hill's corps had not followed Ewell's corps down the valley toward Harrisburg. Instead they had turned east toward Gettysburg, so one would conclude that if their leader did likewise, then his destination was truly Baltimore and Washington.

At this momentous occasion at Center Square stood a young Chambersburg native, Benjamin S. Huber. Beside Huber was a prominent citizen and author, Jacob Hoke, author of the book The Great

<u>Invasion of 1863</u>. Hoke related to the younger man:

"There, Ben is perhaps the most important council in the history of the war, and the fate of the government may depend on it. If General Lee goes down the valley then Harrisburg and Philadelphia are threatened; if he turns east, Baltimore and Washington are in danger, and the government ought to know which way he goes as soon as possible. To this Huber replied: 'Well I have just got back from Harrisburg and I am tired, but as soon as he starts so I can see which way he goes, I will be off again for Harrisburg.' In a short time the council between the two generals ended, and Hill falling back and Lee riding in advance, the whole cavalcade moved forward. Reaching nearly the middle of the diamond where the road leading to Harrisburg is crossed at right angles by the pike leading to Gettysburg and Baltimore, Lee drew the right-hand rein and his horse turned eastward. Looking around for Huber, I saw him elbowing his way through the crowd of citizens to convey this important information to Harrisburg."

Huber, avoiding the Confederate guards and watches, passed from Chambersburg to Roxbury through Dothan Valley, into Amberson Valley, into Perry County and Germantown. He then left Germantown for Newport some forty miles away. Huber arrived in Newport at 3:30 a.m. the following morning, riding this distance in seven hours without dismounting. With Harrisburg being a mere 27 miles away, the Pennsylvania Railroad provided the final link to the capital city. Huber arrived there shortly before daybreak. The Honorable D. W. Rowe met Huber and immediately conducted him to the Capital.

Huber was ushered into a room and found he was in the presence of Couch, General W. F. Smith, and Governor A. C. Curtain.

"After declaring the vital information that he possessed, he was placed through a close examination by Smith. Finally, the General stated: 'Well, gentlemen, the information this young man brings is of the utmost importance, if we can rely on it.' William McClellan Esq. at that time a prominent attorney in Chambersburg, with whom I was well acquanted, happening to be present, said: 'Gentlemen, I know this young man; you can rely on every word he says.' After a short consultation between the Governor and the military men,

dispatches were hurriedly written, and the telegraph operators in the room were set to work. As Mr. Huber arose to leave, the Governor took him by the hand and thanked him for the information that he had brought. The authorities at Washington were aware on Saturday the 27th, that Lee had passed through Chambersburg the day previous, and had gone east. It is not fair to suppose that this important fact was made known to them by the message carried by Mr. Huber."

Lee himself remained in Chambersburg and established his headquarters on the eastern edge of town along the pike leading to Gettysburg. This beautiful location was known as Messersmith's Woods and Lee with his staff remained there from Friday, June 26th until Tuesday morning the 30th. Here councils of war were held, reports received and dispatched to the vast Southern Army, and there the General planned his attack on the Capital of the Commonwealth of Pennsylvania.

Longstreet, on Monday, June 29th, was likewise at his headquarters near Chambersburg. At this point Lee had no valid information on the movement of the Federal forces. In fact, he did not know whether or not their forces had left Virginia.

While at Culpeper, a trusty scout had been sent to Longstreet by Seddon. His mission was to enter the Federal lines, discover the policies, and report the information as soon as it was available. When Longstreet was asked by the scout where he should report, he informed the scout to report to him whenever he had information.

"I reached Chambersburg on the evening of June 27th. At this point, on the night of the 29th, information was received by which the whole plan of the campaign was changed. At ten o'clock that night, Colonel Sorrell, my aide was awakened by an orderly, who reported that a suspicious person had just been arrested by the Provost Marshall. Upon investigation, Sorrell discovered that the suspicious person was the scout, Harrison, that I had sent out at Culpeper. He was dirty, stained, travel worn, and very much broken down. After questing him sufficiently, Colonel Sorrell brought him to my headquarters, and awoke me. He gave me information that the enemy had crossed the Potomac, marched northwest, and that the head of this column was at Frederick City on our right. I felt that the head of this information was exceedingly important, and might involve a change in the

direction of our match. *General Lee had already issued orders that we were to advance toward Harrisburg. I at once sent the scout to General Lee's headquarters and followed him myself early in the morning. I found the General up, and asked him if the information brought by the scout might not involve a change of direction of the head of our column to the right. He immediately acquiesced in the suggestion, possibly saying that he had already given orders to that effect. The movement toward the enemy was begun at once."*

Huber and Harrison are not household names while one discusses the Civil War. However, these courageous men, possessing unknown names and faces, played vital roles in the consolidation of two great armies around Gettysburg.

Meade had corresponded with Reynolds that intelligence from Couch (in Harrisburg) and troop movement from Buford indicated a concentration of the Southern Army either at Chambersburg or on a line bisecting Heidlersburg and York. Meade informed Reynolds that he did not have sufficient data to decide whether it was best to attack before he knew definitely Lee's point of concentration. If the enemy took the offense, Meade would, as the situation now stood, withdraw his army and form a line of battle behind Pipe Creek, between Manchester and Middleburg, Maryland.

Although some have determined that this action would not have been in the best interest of the Union, let us examine why Meade, after careful analysis, may have chosen the Pipe Creek area. First, this area would provide complete cover for Washington and Baltimore no matter the direction from which Lee would advance. It would thereby satisfy the first priority of the powers in the Capital which made Washington's protection forever foremost in any battle plan. Second, Westminster, which would become Meade's base, would be directly behind him, with its short rail connection to Baltimore. Westminster had a complex hub of roads leading in all directions. Hence, this location had the same strategic value for Meade that Gettysburg held for Lee. The added direct routes, either by land or rail, would be of a decided advantage to Meade and the North. Third, the Pipe Line would not be easily turned by Lee, unless he exposed his own army to great danger. Likewise, if the South tried to loop around the Union lines in order to attack Washington and /or Baltimore, the

Army of the Potomac would be intact and near to defend them. Hence, Meade could develop a strong line behind Pipe Creek and place his army with the perfect option for actions in all directions. Without good intelligence or communications, Lee would have to scatter his army in order to subsist it and so expose it to Meade. Lee could unite his army on a course which Meade could compel by simple demonstrations. The decision then for Lee would have been to attack Meade in his chosen position, or retreat without a battle. Also of great importance to the North was the fact that this line would save a great deal of hard marching for Meade's troops. It also would have restored the ranks of thousands of stragglers who did not reach Gettysburg in time for the battle.

To project Meade's thinking to it's final phase, if the Union were to suffer defeat, their line of withdrawal would have been short, and easily covered. Lee in return, would have to make two marches through open country before reaching the mountain passes.

Meade believed his army and that of Lee's to be of comparable size. In this light, Meade's thinking was excellent and the Pipe Creek position an outstanding one for the Army of the Potomac. However, the events of July 1, 1863 drastically altered all plans in relation to the Pipe Creek position and Meade immediately resolved to fight the Confederacy around Gettysburg.

"It is noted before Meade received Hancock's written report from Cemetery Hill, General Meade received additional information as to the state of affairs at the front. His troops were set in motion for Gettysburg, afterward he urged them to forced marches, and under his orders I gave the necessary instructions to the Artillery Reserve and Park for a battle there. The move was, under the circumstances, a bold one, and Meade, as we shall see took great risks."

The General left Taneytown at 11:p.m. and reached the field after midnight.

Lee saw no option except to do battle. If defeat came it would be more disastrous to Meade and less to himself (Lee) at Gettysburg than any point to the east of it. Lee had the South Mountains close to his rear which could be held at a small force. This fact would insure a safe withdrawal, if need be, through the Cumberland Valley. Once the army was through these passes, they would be near the banks of the Potomac. The point of crossing for his army had already been prepared. If Lee pushed eastward to do battle - i.e. to the Pipe Creek area - he would lose these strategic advantages. This Lee could ill afford. He had decided to attack the Union forces. Meade had read correctly. On the morning of July 2, the Union Army and it's "Fishhook" would be ready.

Chapter 11

Before leaving the day of July 1, 1863, we must examine those events that transpired and were related to the final days of the encounter - Thursday and Friday - July 2nd and 3rd. It is to be noted that while under the command of Hooker, the Army of the Potomac had marched 54 miles in two days from Fairfax, Virginia to Frederick, Maryland. The weather was hot and humid; at dusk on July 1, the Army, through forced marches ordered by General Meade, was still coming onto the field. This process and consolidation would continue until Thursday afternoon. The unification of the forces was of paramount importance, even though the added burden to the men could be hazardous. The Army of Northern Virginia was well rested and prepared for battle.

When Henry Raison, Company B, 7th Tennessee, fell on the skirmish line at Willoughby's Run, he became the initial casualty of the battle. The Confederates engaged 30,000 troops; the Federals had 14,000 at their disposal. During this day, the great ability of the Union forces against those heavy odds definitely made the events of Thursday and Friday a reality.

It is interesting to note that a Pennsylvania regiment, the 56th, opened the infantry fighting on Wednesday. In the First Corps were twelve Pennsylvanian organizations; five were also to be found in the Eleventh Corps, with eighteen more in the Twelfth and Third Corps.

As stated earlier, the first day of this Civil War battle was a series of events where two armies by chance, luck, or other means happened to collide north and west of the little town called Gettysburg. It seems to be that there was no surprise, no accident, and certainly no easy going for either side. Buford's Cavalry was not on a training mission. He had been ordered by Meade to go forth and find the enemy and then determine, if, in fact, the Army of Northern Virginia had consolidated near Gettysburg.

WILLIAM "BUZZ" SHANK

Buford sent word that Cemetery Ridge was the location from which to fight the battle. Reynolds and Howard had confirmed this fact. Hancock approved their appraisal. Warren too, found that they were right and Meade promptly gave orders for the concentration of the Army of the Potomac at this place.

This day had marked the great loss of Meade's close friend, Major General John F. Reynolds of Lancaster, Pennsylvania. This man, loved by his troops, would be greatly missed by the Union.

" *The death of Reynolds led Meade to do an act which exhibited his best qualities as a commander. Himself but three days at the head of the Army, selected General Hancock, who left his division to take command of a corps, and sent him to assume the command of the left wing in succession to Reynolds. The result justified the choice, but to make it required courage, insight into character, and rapidity. Even though Hancock was junior in rank to Howard, Meade still made the decision. Hancock on his arrival at the front did just the work that was needed - rallying the troops, addressing and encouraging them, assigning positions to those already there, hastening into line the fresh troops as they arrived."*

Meade stated, *"Reynolds was the noblest as well as the bravest gentleman in the Army."* Those who fought on the first day at Gettysburg should receive special glory for repulsing an army of superior numbers, thus securing valuable time for the arrival and concentration of the rest of the Union Army.

The accomplishments of General John Buford and his Cavalry during the first day's battle, cannot be overlooked. Buford, a Kentuckian, was a skilled Indian fighter on the frontier. He soon developed the philosophy that by using the sabre, one's chances of survival was greatly diminished. Buford was responsible for the introduction of new tactics to the Union Cavalry at a place called Thoroughfare Gap. The Cavalry would rush a position, stop, and three horsemen would dismount and fight as infantry soldiers while the fourth man held the reins of the horses. They would then rapidly remount and speed to another location. These tactics were employed at the Second Battle of Bull Run, when 3,000 troops held at bay, a Confederate force of 27,000 for six hours. Buford's men utilized these procedures west of Gettysburg and against great odds, gave the Union precious time and prevented what may have been a disaster. The concentration of Lee's Army was delayed and gave Meade valuable time to hasten his troops onward to Gettysburg.

As the battle of the first day ended, Meade was still at a decided disadvantage. The whole of the Union forces had not converged as yet on Gettysburg. Missing were brigades of the 3rd Corps, the 2nd Corps, the 5th and 6th Corps, while the majority of the Union Calvary was not at Gettysburg. The brave men of the 1st and 11th Corps had sustained 10,000 killed, wounded, captured, or missing on this very day. The fighting had ceased and the calm and quiet of the evening was a welcomed respite. It should be noted that from approximately 2:00 to 4:30 p.m., the 26th North Carolinians had over 800 in line at the start of hostilities. In the ensuing two and one half hours, their losses and wounded amounted to 588. On July 4, this brave group of men had 80 present for duty. This is the largest record of losses sustained by either a Union or Confederate regiment during the Civil War. In this sequence of fighting, the 24th Michigan lost 363, the 151st

Pennsylvania lost 337, and the 149th Pennsylvania lost 336. The entire Color Guard of the 24th Michigan were killed or wounded. Their flag was carried by nine persons in succession - four were killed and four were wounded.

Then under cover of a full moon, the Federal soldiers, under the guidance of their Commander and the direction of skilled engineers, worked , "dug in," built breastworks (especially on the right flank at Culp's Hill), until their position was made too strong to be carried by direct assault. Under Meade's direction, reinforcements were made along the entire line and preparations for battle were completed. Being an engineer and a man that strived for perfection, Meade, although exhausted like his troops, worked throughout the night to prepare for Thursday morning.

Meade clearly understood the strength and advantages of his position. He knew that Lee did not have the luxury of time on his side. After his first day, the Confederates were ecstatic and boastful. *"In Gettysburg that evening July 1, the streets were ribbons of Confederate grey. Professor Michael Jacobs recounts, that portion of (Major General Robert E.) Rhodes division which lay down before our dwelling . . . was greatly elated with the results of the first day's battle. And the same may be said of the whole Rebel Army. They were anxious to engage in conversation - to communicate their views and feelings, and to elicit ours. They were boastful of themselves, of their cause, and the skill of their officers, and were anxious to tell us of the unskillful manner in which some of our officers had conducted the fight which had just closed. When informed that General Archer and 1500 of his men had been captured, they said; 'Tomorrow we will take all these back again; and, having already taken 5000 prisoners of you today, we will take the balance of your men tomorrow.' Having been well fed, provisioned, and rested, and successful on this day, their confidence knew no bounds . . . to us it seemed as if the Rebels would be able to accomplish their boasts. We were disheartened, and almost in despair."*

Also to their advantage was the knowledge that the Federal troops were tired from the long forced marches in hot, humid conditions to reach the field. They felt that their task may be an easy one. The Union line had now become a concave three miles in length. It reached from the Round Tops on the left to Culp's Hill on the right flank and would now be known as the "Fish Hook." By choosing this ground to do battle, Meade had developed several advantages. First, he held the majority of the high ground and its rugged terrain. Second, Lee wanted to pick the site and Longstreet had urged a defensive position. But Lee was forced from those thoughts on how the battle would be fought - he now would become the aggressor. Thirdly, the Union would be able to move men and supplies quickly inside their compact position while the enemy would labor in their convex battle line that was miles in length.

Finally came the dawn, then the cooling morning into the noonday. Time moved into the afternoon and still no activity on the part of the Confederates. Some felt that these events, along with the beautiful moonlit night of Wednesday, were the cause of divine intervention on behalf of the Union. The 2nd, 5th, and 6th Corps were given adequate time to come onto the field and most important, the Northern soldiers were given hours of vital rest. Around 4 p.m. on Thursday, the 6th Corps, under the Command of General John Sedwick came onto the field with 15,400 troops.

These men had marched 35 miles since 7 pm the previous evening to reach Gettysburg.

"A great deal has been written about the theories of Lee and Longstreet concerning this battle around Gettysburg. This subject will not be scrutinized in great detail. It would be appropriate to state that Lee's blood was up and his determination to attack Meade's Army was to become the order of the day. There could and would be no retreat. The Union was in front of our position and the attack would not be delayed. Longstreet believed that the Southern Army should swing around Meade's left flank and then adopt a defensive position. Thus perversely does the fate of battles hinge on the turn of the wheel. Here was Longstreet, Lee's most experienced Corps Commander, proposing in effect that Lee move into the very position for defense (The Big Pipe Creek Area), the occupancy of which had so obsessed Meade's mind until a few hours before; while Meade himself planning a defensive battle, had preempted the Longstreet thesis and was getting set to do a Fredericksburg in reverse by encouraging the Confederates to pound themselves to death against the hard anvil of Cemetery Ridge *and the Round Tops."*

During the valuable time that showed no initiative from the Southern Army, the Union positions were rechecked. Hunt had completed a careful inspection on Cemetery Hill. At approximately 4:30, the action commenced. Sickles 3rd Corps, without informing the adjacent 2nd Corps Commander Hancock, moved forward, against orders, to the so called high ground. The gap, as detected by Warren on Little Round Top, was as yet not filled. Likewise, the fighting commenced in the Peach Orchard, The Wheatfield, Devil's Den, and The Valley of Death. *"General Meade has been nearly continuously on the field, making strenuous exertions for establishing the line, in person bringing up and placing reinforcements, exposing himself in the reckless manner dictated by the emergency, during which he had his faithful old horse, Baldy shot out from under him."*

Although Sickles erred, Meade did not abandon him or back down from his responsibility. He saw that this 3rd Corps must be reinforced and backed immediately. He directed Hunt to bring up reserve batteries. Caldwell's division of the 2nd Corps, divisions from the 5th Corps, and men from the 1st and 12th Corps from the extreme right were pressed into action. The onslaught by the enemy continued, however, each time troops were hurled into the action at the right time. Meade was in the center of it all and showed that he possessed those qualities that were necessary to command a great army. At that moment, he received the trust and respect of his men. General E.P. Alexander of the Confederate Artillery Corp commented on the leadership of Meade. *"Meade saw the danger, and with military foresight prepared to meet it with every available man. There was not during the war a finer example of efficient command than that displayed by Meade on this occasion. He immediately began to bring to the scene reinforcements, both of infantry and artillery, from every corps and from every part of the line . . . His work that afternoon presents perhaps the best example which the war produced of active supervision and efficient handling of a large force on the defense."*

Meade, having ordered Newton to bring up Robinson and Doubleday to fill this gap to the left of the 2nd Corps, is back on the field. Gibbon's line becomes heavily engaged and the action in the area becomes intense. Meanwhile, Meade and a few aides are waiting near this crucial gap. The area is beginning to fill with shot and shell. *"At this moment, Meade at a short distance off, a line of the enemy making straight for the gap. Will nothing stop these people? He glances anxiously at the cemetery, whence help should come. It will be a disaster unless something can stop these troops, if only for a brief space of time. The General realizes the situation but too well. He straightens himself in his stirrups, as do also the aides who now ride close to him, bearing themselves up to meet the crisis. It is in the minds of those who follow him that he is going to throw himself into the breach - anything to gain a few minutes time. Suddenly someone cries out, 'There they come General!' and looking to the right, Newton is seen galloping in advance of Doubleday's Division, followed by Robinson. Amid wild excitement and shouting the Divisions fall into line, Meade rides ahead with the skirmish line, waving his hat, saying to those about him, 'come on, gentlemen', and someone remarking that it seemed at one time pretty desperate, it is pleasant to hear him reply in his hearty way: 'Yes, but it is all right now, it is all right now.'"*

It must be noted that troops from the right flank and other points were rushed to strengthen lines during the epic struggles on July 2. This was made possible by the Fish Hook concept and the Commander, who for the first time on behalf of the Union forces, was on site directing troops to the areas in need and filling any gap immediately.

Of special note was the intense fighting on Culp's Hill. Early during day two when little activity was evidenced on the part of the Confederates, General Alpheus S. Williams commanded his boys to dig ditches and erect breastworks. The General, a West Pointer, was going by the book. The weather was hot and muggy. Rest would have been more welcome than this unpopular directive. However, this preparation would prove to be invaluable during the remainder of the day and the final day of the campaign. In addition, the tenacious fighting of these men on the hill was evidenced by the will of General George S. Greene. With grave danger on the left flank, Greene and one division was given the grave responsibility of holding this position. Now the ditches and breastworks, completed by the men of the 12th Corps, would be put to their proper use. Greene's men had barely occupied their positions when the enemy commenced the attack. The time was 7 pm.

For two hours the Rebels stormed this hill and were repulsed by Greene's troops and the 1st Corps. Howard and Wadsworth responded to the call for assistance and returned to Culp's Hill with three regiments to solidify the right flank.

Meanwhile on the left flank, the Union forces were desperately striving to place their troops in positions that would repel the impending onslaught by the Confederates. Until the fighting will subside, the names of Vincent, O'Rorke, Chamberlain, and Crawford will be long remembered.

While the 3rd Brigade of Barne's Division was enroute, Colonel Strong Vincent rode ahead to Little Round Top and selected the best position for his men. His selection was most important and a vital cog in the preservation of the left flank. If Vincent had not acted so quickly and decisively, the Rebels who were making their way through the woods, would have gained control of this pivotal point in the Union line. Colonel Joshua Lawrence

⊔namberlain, Commander of the 20th Maine, was in the lead and scaled the eastern slope of the hill and swung around to assume a southern posture. Simultaneously, Colonel Patrick H. O'Rorke, a fine West Pointer, and friend of Warren, in command of the 140th New York, came on the field and came in line with the troops of Vincent and Chamberlain. The ensuing engagement is all but legendary in Civil War history. The brave men who fought this day under these Commanders, saved the left flank and the possibility of a Union defeat. As the day wore down and the fighting subsided, it appeared that the Rebels would make one last charge on Little Round Top. Wofford's Brigade, bolstered by Longstreet's presence, mounted this final charge. Union troops had been crowded against the base of the hill. On the northern crest, stood the Pennsylvania Reserves, eager to dash into battle on their native soil. As Wofford's men rushed across the fields toward Little Round Top, Crawford determined the time had come and felt his troops could meet the Rebels "halfway." He grabbed a battle-flag while General William McCandless did likewise and with a blood curdling yell, the command was given to charge down the hill and engage the enemy. Through the bushes and the piles of dead and wounded, the division ran as if swept forward by an irresistible force. The Confederates were checked and ran back through The Wheatfield and into the next woods. The fighting on the left flank had ended; the 6th Corps came on to the field, and the Fish Hook of the Union remained intact.

As evening turned into night, the cry of the wounded could be heard throughout the field. The heat remained staggering as the men called for water. *"Help me - please bring water."* Soldiers looked for their fallen comrades. The dead, after this day, became a significant figure - including the many horses that were slain.

The respective commanders were now engaged in preparation for the day that would follow - Friday July 3. Lee was still optimistic. He felt Meade was forced to weaken his position in the middle to support the left flank. He knew the morale of his veteran soldiers remained high. Besides, a large number of the Southern forces had not been engaged during day two. His blood continued to run high and this army of destiny could not fail. His men basically were rested and perhaps tomorrow would be the better day. Then Lee was reminded that Longstreet no longer had "one boot off" - Pickett and his entire division had arrived at Gettysburg. Add to that the fact that Stuart and the Southern Cavalry was now whole and at his disposal. Yes, Lee felt the next day would be their victory.

Meanwhile, Meade recalled troops and restored a proper balance along the entire Union line. Sedgwick and the powerful 6th Corps were now up and ready to be engaged. The Union boys had just repelled the enemy on both their right and left flanks. These men had solidified themselves as a determined and engaging foe. Their spirits had been lifted. They now knew that their Commander was available to place reserves in weakened spots immediately and maintain a harmony in the lines while the battle continued. At his headquarters, Meade called a conference of his Generals and advisors to contemplate strategy for the following day. After posing several possibilities for discussion, the group debated the options. Meade had very little to say. The consensus was the Army would remain in place tomorrow, not attack, and stay in place this one day before attacking.

Meade then spoke and told those present that the orders had already been issued to remain in place and do battle. He was glad that his views coincided with their conclusions. As the men left his headquarters, Meade called General John Gibbon to his side. He informed the General that, in his opinion, the Rebels would attack the Union center tomorrow in front of his position. Gibbon assured the General that he and his men would be ready and waiting. Some say that the fates were kind to Meade. I'm sure that Meade would like to have thought that his experience and the flow of battle during days one and two brought him to his conclusion. It always seems so easy when one knows the answer before hand. Like you and I, Meade did not enjoy that luxury. Meade ordered Hunt to realign his artillery and focus heavily on the central portion of the line. It is interesting to note that on day three, Hunt utilizes only 80 cannons, while the Southern artillery fired 120 weapons.

The final day of the battle around Gettysburg was envisioned by Lee as the day the South would be victorious. He felt that Meade was vulnerable at the center. The strategy was to simultaneously attack the Union's right flank and center, while the Cavalry would swing behind the Union lines and attack its middle from the rear.

Meade had analyzed the two previous days and came to the conclusion that the focal point of Lee's attack would indeed be the center of the Union lines. His preparations were exacting and immediate. His orders brought in fresh troops and equipment along the entire Union line. At the center, all arrangements were completed to have these fresh soldiers nearby on the Taneytown Road, plus ample quantities of ammunition available.

"Moreover, Meade had so shrewdly anticipated the movements of the foe that he had massed his entire infantry in great strength in the rear of Hancock, to be ready for whatever crisis might develop during the afternoon. These plans were so magnificently carried out that when the closing phases of the fight began to open up, nothing was needed except to fill in with fresh guns the vacancies occasioned by batteries which had to be withdrawn on account of damage, or to be restocked with grape and canister. Hardly a brigade of infantry needed to change its place in view of

the cannonade and the last charge. *This prescient generalship shown by Meade has never been fully appreciated. It was one of the signal marks of his ability in the battle."*

Other factors began to unfold. Early Friday morning, Kane's Brigade of Geary's Division attacked the Rebel at the light of day. This surprise movement, on the Union's right flank, caught the Southerners off guard, thus eliminating a consolidated attack of the Union right and center as planned by Lee. The fighting was fierce on Culp's Hill and lasted from 4:00 a.m. until 11:00 a.m. The Rebels experienced heavy losses as the Union will was imposed during this engagement. This fighting was regarded as the most obstinate and deadly of the war. *"The slain were lying literally in heaps. In front of Geary's position were more Confederate dead than the entire list of causalities in the whole 12th Corps. Human beings, mangled and torn, in every manner, from a shot through the body or head to bodies torn to pieces by exploding shells, were everywhere. The Stonewall Brigade, like the Louisiana Tigers the evening before, had met their match. Their reputation for invincible courage was unimpeached, but the stone-wall this time stood in their way, and they had to yield to the inevitable. At eleven o'clock the battle ceased, and the Federal line was once more intact."*

SILENCE AND REST PREVAILED
FROM 11:00 AM UNTIL 1:00 PM

"The warmth and humidity of the afternoon engulfed the field. The quiet seemed to make the men more comfortable as they rested and waited. What next? The men in grey were aware as they scurried hither and fro. Can't be late! This is the day. Everything must be ready for the big parade. There seemed to be no fear on either side: just a subtle determination for this great event that was about to unfold.

What was that sound? We hear so many guns. What was that? A signal gun or two on Seminary Ridge, you say. It is barely ten minutes past one o'clock and the silence is broken. Suddenly, as if a tidal wave had crashed upon the shore, the terrific fire of one hundred and twenty Confederate guns roar. Screaming projectiles pour through the sunlit air and descend upon man, horse, caisson, and everything in their way. There was shot and shell

138

as the iron rained down upon the Union center. Cover - take cover! The Union guns are now in full reply.

"Union Captain Samuel Fiske was at the center as a member of Hancock's Corps. He observed, 'It is touching to see the little birds, all out of their wits with fright, flying wildly about amidst the tornado of terrible missiles, and uttering strange notes of distress. It was touching to see the innocent cows and calves, feeding in the fields, torn to pieces by the shells. . . It was a nobler sight to see the sublime bravery of our gallant Artillerists, serving their guns with the utmost precision and coolness. Knowing they were the mark aimed at by equally brave and skillful enemy, and clinging on their beloved pieces to the bitter end.'

Hunt's artillery was ever vigilant and their moments of glory were rapidly approaching. Although having a limited number of weapons their strategic positioning would prove vital. Immediately over the knoll, Meade's headquarters takes a severe pounding from the Rebel fire. Man and animal are killed. The General and his aides are spared and have advanced to a safer location. Still the cannonade continues. The frightening sound passes from one half to now a full hour. The guns continue to talk and as they do, the Southern casualities begin to mount. How does this affect the thousand upon thousands of foot soldiers who will soon form those long colorful lines of the big parade? Over one hour has passed and yet neither side has decided to pause. Will it ever end?

The smoke between the opposing armies becomes a viable force. It can aid the Confederates. like their wooded position. Together Meade and Hunt reach the same conclusion. Silence the Union artillery - conserve ammunition. Regroup damaged weapons and place damaged batteries together. Bring up the reserve units to replace any heavy casualties. Soon thereafter, the Southern artillery stayed silent. Have we destroyed the Union guns or have they simply used all of their ammunition? The smoke , the smoke, if we could only see. Then suddenly, a gentle western breeze began to break the cover of the smoke. At first at the lower level and then higher on the ridge, the cry went up - 'Here they come'. The reclining artillery men jumped to their feet, ready for action. The footsoldier picked himself up and hurried himself back into the line. The time had come.

Fredericksburg, surely passed through the minds of the veteran Union forces as the enemy came closer and closer.

As the silent guns held their posture after the eventful cannonade, men, by the thousands, came into view from those woods and the low spots on the Rebel right flank. Aligned in all their splendor, row upon row, regiment after regiment, their colors flying, they came forward as if enlightened by a grand parade. Yes, these are the identical soldiers that professor Jacobs and his son Henry observed from the garret window of their downtown residence.

Their objective was the small clump of trees approximately one mile away. Bravely, unwavering, they proceeded. In eight short minutes, they would approach the Emmitsburg Road and the two stone fences to be crossed in pursuit of their goal. There's Pickett's proud division on the left. Armistead, Garnett, and Trimble are there - ever moving forward. The horsemen gallop up an down among the men as the gun barrels glisten in the afternoon sun. Through the wheat and corn, magnificent, as if one, they come. Then the guns, the explosions, the hurt, the death. The long lines are no longer there.

Regiments disappear in the wink of an eye. There is no longer the beauty that characterized these men but a few minutes ago."

As Pickett's Charge comes to it's climax, Union newsman, Charles Carleton Coffin wrote the descriptive and haunting words:

"Pandemonium was everywhere. The rule. Men fire into each other's faces not five feet apart. There are bayonet thrusts, sabre strokes, pistol shots; cool deliberate movements on the part of some - hot passionate, desperate efforts with others; hand-to-hand contests; recklessness of life; tenacity of purpose; fiery determination; oaths, yells, curses, hurrahs, shouting; throwing out their guns, gulping up blood, falling - legless, armless, headless. There are ghastly heaps of dead men. Seconds are centuries, minutes ages.

The Rebel column has lost its power. The lines waver. The soldiers on the front rank look around for their supporters. They are gone - fleeing over the field, broken, shattered, thrown into confusion by the remorseless fire . . . The lines have disappeared like a straw in a candle's flame. The ground is thick with the dead, and the wounded are like the withered leaves of autumn. Thousands of

Rebels throw down their arms and give themselves up as prisoners.

Thirty minutes has elapsed. The fight is done. The silence returns amidst the moans and cries of the wounded. One can barely see for the lingering smoke hanging over the field once again.

Yet the final tale is still to be told. Simultaneously to Pickett's Charge, East and to the rear of the Union center, four Confederate Cavalry Brigades led by General Jeb Stuart engage three Union Brigades under the leadership of General David McM. Gregg. The day could rest on the outcome of this engagement. Although outnumbered, Gregg had at his disposal General George A. Custer and Colonels J. Irvin Gregg and John B. McIntosh. These were determined men. After artillery and rifle fire were exchanged across an open field, the battle lines were drawn. The combined four brigades of Generals Wade Hampton and Fitz Hugh Lee and Colonels J.R. Chambliss and A.G. Jenkins developed the general Southern fight plan of closed columns, sabres flashing and the customary 10 alignment. As they advanced, they took heavy fire. At this point, Custer's Brigade received orders from Gregg to charge. The opposing forces approached one another at full gallop, horses were overturned as the battle raged on. There were charges and counter charges and the Federals executed effective flanking attacks. The fine resistance plus the pistol and sabre work of the Union Cavalry demoralized the forces of Stuart. The soldiers separated with the Southern men returning to the ridge from whence they began. The Gregg forces were now in complete control of the field of battle. Stuart and his men returned to the Southern lines at the rear of Seminary Ridge. This desperate Cavalry engagement was over. Casualties were heavy and the fighting was called some of the fiercest in the entire war. The Union Cavalry would never again play, "second fiddle" to the Rebel forces."

Meade had been in command of the Union forces just six days. The battle around Gettysburg was concluded. The South had reached it's "High Water Mark" on their final thrust during Pickett's Charge. After such a struggle, it would seem proper that the wounded should be attended to as quickly as possible and the dead buried whenever appropriate. General Meade rode from the Union right to a position at the Little Round Top amid the cheers of his fellow comrades. His purpose was to send out probes to determine the position and attitude of the enemy. It was quickly ascertained the the Rebel Artillery was still positioned along Seminary Ridge, perhaps hoping for a Union advance. Over half of the Southern forces were just one-half mile from where the great charge began. Among them were the Divisions of Hood and McLaws. The big question was never answered: Did Lee order these troops in to support Pickett's men? Lee later answered - Yes; Longstreet replied - No. Meade in all this uncertainty, could not make a false step at this critical time. If he did , disaster could be the result. *"He had to decide, not simply for the time, nor for the Army under his command, but for the whole country, for the Government, and for all time to come."*

It is important to understand that armies of this size did not instantaneously go from a defensive mode to offense. Communications would not allow this type of rapid transition. Reconnaissance was vital and necessary. Meade had concluded that too many fresh troops and artillery would await him and he could create a reversal of the famous charge. Time was an important and realistic factor. Losses had to be assessed, regiments and divisions regrouped, and the men and artillery rearmed. It would conclude with decisions on the proper tactics to employ. The day was late and his men had fought a brilliant battle. Meade decided not to charge into the unknown, but to enjoy the great victory with his Commanders and his men. He made the right decision.

On the morning of July 4, General Barlow, after a 5 a.m. inspection, reported to Meade that the Southern withdrawal was nothing more than an effort to deceive. The directive was sent out to all Union Commanders to rest the men, those men who had just completed long marches and three days of fierce fighting. Battle lines were not to be changed. Regroup and rearm those under one's command. Burial parties were to be formed and all the enemy dead, in the vicinity of their lines, were to be buried. The despondent and demoralized Army of Northern Virginia remained on the field at Gettysburg through Saturday, July 4. Perhaps by waiting, they were hoping that the Army of the Potomac might charge and give these defeated men an opportunity to avenge their great losses.

It is important to note that the mood and conscience of the Southern leadership had undergone a transformation. Even with their army intact, they no longer expressed the great desire to dislodge Meade and his troops from their positions. There were no great aspirations for renewal of the fighting.

Lee had given the orders to General John D. Imboden to start with the wounded, by way of Cashtown straits toward Virginia. It started to rain at noon on Saturday and continued through July 5, making most roads impassable. The Southern injured, riding in springless wagons experienced the discomfort of the aftermath of war. Any wagon that incurred difficulties was to be placed at the side of the road and abandoned. Scarcely one individual in a hundred was receiving medical attention. The wounded in the wagons had been without food for the past thirty hours. There was no straw, no comforts for the long trip home. Many would not complete the journey. This wagon train as observed by individuals in the area was quoted as being seventeen miles long. The wounded and walking wounded were estimated at between ten and twelve thousand men.

Seven thousand, five hundred and forty, were left dead or wounded on the field of battle. Lee's retreat was underway, and there would be no stopping them now.

EPILOGUE

HIS COUNTRY HAD CALLED, THE WAR WAS NOT GOING WELL. Defeat had become the by product for the Army of the Potomac. Yet, as if designed by God himself, the right man, a man of clear mind, intellect, courage and a General not immersed on the political ladder to success, stepped forward to assume command.

When this epic battle concluded, one cannot help but think that Lee recognized that the inevitable was beginning to unfold. Perhaps, more importantly, the "everyday" soldier must have been acutely aware of the impending consequences - the road would now become harder to travel and the great victories would almost become the figment of one's imagination.

Meade had transformed the mind and spirit of the Union forces. He proved that their character could be changed into a most viable entity, the Cavalry no longer played second fiddle to the Confederates, and the men by being in the right place accomplished feats far beyond all expectations. The battle became the supreme crisis in our country's history and the turning point in its destiny.

John Boyle of the 111th Pennsylvania Volunteers recorded his thoughts concerning the General. *"His mind was highly trained and logical, and his temperament was impetuous. He possessed great natural dignity, and an innate and lofty pride, a vigorous conscience, an unyielding will. He lacked the magnetism that excites superficial applause, but embodied the greatness and fidelity that inspire respect and attract worth. It is said that his ear was so well trained that, awakened at night by distant firing, he could tell in an instant whence the sound proceeded and what troops were engaged, and that his eye for topography was so skilled that onlooking at a range of hills he could describe the nature of the ground beyond them, and tell where the streams were and in what direction they flowed. When the struggle ended, Lee said of him that he feared him more than any man he had ever met in battle."*

Frank Aretas Haskell, a Union Officer, served at Gettysburg on the staff of General John Gibbon and the 2nd Corps. He was an eye witness of the battle and the actions of the Union Commander. His tactics and movement of the army were observed until the climactic open field advance on the final day. Mr. Haskell penned his thoughts and observations two weeks after the epic conflict around Gettysburg.

"The Providence of God had been with us - we ought not to have doubted it - General Meade commanded the Army of the Potomac. I now felt that we had a clear-headed, honest soldier, to command the army, who would do his best always - that there would be no repetition of Chancellorsville. Meade was not as much known in the Army as many of the other Corps Commanders, but the officers who knew, all thought highly of him, a man of great modesty, with none of those qualities which are noisy and assuming, and hankering for cheap newspaper fame. I happened to know much of General Meade - he and General Gibbon had always been very intimate, and I have seen much of him - I think my own notions concerning General Meade at this time, were shared quite generally by the army."

Lt. Haskell realized that in any war skillful leadership and good fighting were the prerequisites. He knew that these elements, not mere number, would determine the outcome at

Gettysburg.

"The magnitude of the armies engaged, the number of casualties, the object sought by the Rebel, the result, will all contribute to give Gettysburg a place among the great historical battles of the world. That General Meade's concentration was rapid - over thirty miles a day marched by some of the Corps - that his position was skillfully selected and his dispositions good; that he fought the battle hard and well; that his victory was brilliant and complete, I think all should admit."

Examination of this great battle always has a tendency to concentrate on the fire power of the armies. However, also on the field of battle, the real emotions of courage, leadership, and even greatness became readily apparent. High moral courage marked a few. The point was clear in his 1967 book, <u>At Ease, Stories I Tell to Friends</u>. President and General Dwight David Eisenhower uses as his example, General George Gordon Meade.

"George Gordon Meade was assigned command of the Army of the Potomac only three days before the Battle of Gettysburg commenced. No other

officer through the war was given so little time to prepare himself and his troops for such a climactic engagement.

As he rode toward the battle on July 1, receiving reports that his 1st Corps had been forced back, it's Commanding General killed on the field, the 11th Corps disastrously routed and thousands of his men taken prisoner, Meade's mind must have been torn with anxiety about the future of this army and - for he was only human - occasionally worried about his own fate as its Commander.

When he reached the field after midnight, he pushed himself and his horse through hours of inspection. It might be late in the day before Meade would have enough troops on the field to balance Confederate strength. The morning of July 2, after hardly more than a few hours sleep, he was back on the lines, accompanied only by a staff officer and an orderly. But this simple, cold, serious soldier with his businesslike air did inspire confidence.

For Meade, this was the moment of truth when all within him, particularly his moral courage, had to bear tough and strong on the problems ahead.

No council of war could be called. No delay for leisure study could be permitted by Lee. The decision had to be made. And the decision was solely Meade's responsibility. Then he turned his horse and quietly rode away to issue the orders that would make his decision operative.

In all this, there is neither visible drama nor glamour; only the loneliness of one man on whose mind weighed the fate of ninety thousand comrades and of the Republic they served. Meade's claim to greatness in that moment may very well be best evidenced by the total absence of the theatrical. When thousands of lives were at stake there was no time for postures or declamations." A profound statement made by the Commanding General over one hundred years later - simply a man and his peer.

Yes, George Gordon Meade had taken an unsuccessful army and had won the great victory. Future battles would be characterized by the decided numbers, both in men and material, in the favor of the Union forces. The end of the conflict could now be seen.

Meade once said, *"I like fighting as little as any man."* Yet, at Gettysburg, this Pennsylvanian led his Union forces to victory over a veteran, well rested opponent which boasted of their abilities and their leadership. His President would initially condemn him and rush to the bedside of the political Sickles, proclaiming him the hero of Gettysburg. As this word circulated by newspaper and word of mouth, there were many who became upset at the tactics of their President. One such individual was General Howard, who sent a letter directly to Lincoln. Although not a close friend to Meade, Howard through a sense of fair play, wrote in direct terms to Lincoln:

"Victory at Gettysburg was due mainly to the energetic operations of our Commanding General prior to the engagement, and to the manner in which he handled the troops on the field. The reserves have never been before, during this war, been thrown in at just the right moment. In many cases when points were just being carried by the enemy, a regiment or brigade appeared to stop his progress and hurl him back. Moreover, I have never seen a more hearty co-operation on the part of the General Officers as since General Meade took the Command. He was in favor of an immediate attack at Williamsport, but with the evident

difficulties in our way, the uncertainty of a success, and the strong conviction of our best military minds against the risk, I must say that I think the General acted wisely. We have, if I may be allowed to say it, a Commanding General in whom all the officers with whom I have contact express complete confidence."

Meade never waivered. His dignity, honor, and respect for his fellow Pennsylvanians and countrymen was always preeminent. Perhaps because he was Commander and had prepared himself for this critical time in the nation's history. Meade's words became prophetic when he humbly proclaimed, *"The longer this war continues, the more Gettysburg will be appreciated."*

On October 31, 1872 while on his daily walk with Mrs. Meade at his side, General Meade was attacked with the violent pain in the side of his old wound. It was the second time since the war pneumonia had overtaken him. He died on November 6, 1872, at age 57.

A unique man is gone. His great faith and love of country sustained him. His achievements at Gettysburg are now history. To this man we owe a great debt. He is gone, but he can never be forgotten.

General George G. Meade
Commander of the Army of the Potomac

Picture credit: U.S. Library of Congress

Today the Cupola
on top of the Lutheran Seminary
overlooks a peaceful and busy Gettysburg
150 years later

Picture credit: Judy S. Walter 2013

Gettysburg is appreciated

Picture credit: Penny Maxson 2013

BIBLIOGRAPHY

Angle, Paul N. <u>A Pictorial History of the Civil War Years</u>. New York: Doubleday

Boothe, F. Norton. <u>Great Generals of the Civil War and Their Battles.</u>

Boyle, John B. <u>Soldiers True, The Story of the One Hundred and Eleventh Regiment Pennsylvania Volunteers. 1862-1865</u>. New York: 1903

Bradford, Ned. <u>Battle and Leaders of the Civil War.</u> New York: A Meridan Book, New American Library.

Christian, William. <u>Letters to His Wife.</u>

<u>Civil War Times Illustrated.</u> John E. Stanchak, editor. Harrisburg, Pennsylvania: 1985

Clark, Champ. <u>The Civil War - Gettysburg.</u> Alexandria, Virginia: Time Life Books.

Cleaves, Freeman. <u>Meade of Gettysburg.</u> Norman and London: University of Oklahoma Press.

Coddington, Edwin B. <u>The Gettysburg Campaign.</u> Dayton, Ohio: Morningside Bookshop.

Comte de Paris. <u>The Battle of Gettysburg</u>. Philadelphia: Porter and Coates.

<u>Dedication of the Monuments, Pennsylvania at Gettysburg. Volume 1,</u> William Stanley Ray, State Printer, 1914

DeTrobriand, Regis. <u>Four Years in the Army of the Potomac.</u> Boston: 1889

Dictionary of American Biography. New York: Charles Scribner's and Sons.

Eisenhower, Dwight David. At Ease-Stories I Tell To Friends, New York: Doubleday and Company, Inc., 1967.

Fiske, Samuel. Mr. Dunn Browne's Experiences in the Army. Boston: Nichols and Noyes, 1866.

Haskell, Frank Aretas. The Battle of Gettysburg. Boston: Houghton Mifflin, 1958.

Hoke, Jacob. The Great Invasion of 1863. Dayton, Ohio: The Otterbein Press, 1913.

Inman, Arthur Crew, editor. Soldier of the South, General Pickett's War Letters to His Wife. New York: 1928.

Jacobs, Michael. Notes on the Rebel Invasion and the Battle of Gettysburg. Philadelphia: Lippincott, 1864.

Lincoln and the Civil War in the Diaries and Letters of John Hay. edited by Tyler Bennett. New York: DeCapo Paperbacks, a subsidiary of Plenum Publishing Company.

McPherson, James M. Battle Cry of Freedom. New York: Ballantine Books.

Meade, George Gordon. The Life and Letters of George Gordon Meade. volumes I and II, New York: 1913

Schildt, John W. Roads to Gettysburg. Parsons, West Virginia: McClain Printing Company, 1978.

Shaara, Michael. The Killer Angels. New York: Ballentine Books

Stackpole, Edward J. They Met at Gettysburg. Harrisburg, Pennsylvania: Stackpole Books, 1956.

Storrick, W.C. The Battle of Gettysburg. Gettysburg: Stan Clark Military Books.

Wheeler, Richard. Witness to Gettysburg. New York: Meridan Books, New American Library.

Williams, T. Harry. Lincoln and His Generals. New York: Alfred Knoff, 1952.

Young, Jesse Bowman. The Battle of Gettysburg. New York and London: Harper and Brothers Publishers, 1913.